KT-377-769

Reformation of the Heart

Seasonal Meditations
by a Gay Christian

CHRIS GLASER

Westminster John Knox Press
LOUISVILLE
LONDON • LEIDEN

© 2001 by Chris R. Glaser

All rights reserved. No part of this book may be reproduced or transmitted in any form or by any means, electronic or mechanical, including photocopying, recording, or by any information storage or retrieval system, without permission in writing from the publisher. For information, address Westminster John Knox Press, 100 Witherspoon Street, Louisville, Kentucky 40202-1396.

Scripture quotations, unless otherwise indicated, are from An Inclusive Language Lectionary (based on the Revised Standard Version of the Bible, copyright © 1946, 1952, 1971, and 1973 by the Division of Christian Education of the National Council of the Churches of Christ in the U.S.A. and are used by permission), or from the New Revised Standard Version of the Bible, copyright © 1989 by the Division of Christian Education of the National Council of the Churches of Christ in the U.S.A., and used by permission.

Book design by Sharon Adams
Cover design by Kathy York

First edition
Published by Westminster John Knox Press
Louisville, Kentucky

This book is printed on acid-free paper that meets the American National Standards Institute Z39.48 standard. ∞

PRINTED IN THE UNITED STATES OF AMERICA
01 02 03 04 05 06 07 08 09 10 — 10 9 8 7 6 5 4 3 2 1

Library of Congress Cataloging-in-Publication Data
Glaser, Chris.
    Reformation of the heart : seasonal meditations by a gay Christian /
    Chris Glaser.— 1st ed.
        p. cm.
    Includes index.
    ISBN 0-664-22306-0 (alk. paper)
        1. Church year meditations. 2. Christian gays—Religious life. I. Title.

BV30 .G58 2001
242'.6—dc21   2001017786

To Mom,
Mildred Cronister Glaser,
with love

Contents

A Personal Word

To Mom—Mildred Cronister Glaser

As I look back on all who have shaped my faith and my spirituality, I acknowledge one whose influence has touched me and grown within me far more than any other theologian, minister, or spiritual director. She has blessed me with a sense of belovedness, grace, forgiveness, faith, doubt, and humor. She taught me to read and encouraged my discovery of the world through books. She opened my mind to writers who did not fit our narrow definitions of those who were "saved," but in whose words she saw truth and value and meaning. She opened my heart to "strangers," listening intently to a lonely waitress recently divorced, inviting a man asking for money at our door into our home for bacon and eggs, crying at the pain and suffering she witnessed in books and in films and in the news.

She also taught me how to serve. She's the reason I enjoy fixing a meal for a guest, she's the reason I enjoy being a "domestic engineer" as much as a writer and teacher, she's the reason I enjoy being there for someone who needs to talk. Her own sacrificial service modeled for me how to make personal sacrifices to serve.

She was also the reason I love adventure and pushing beyond boundaries. I have traveled where she only dreamed to go. I have rebelled with the same spunk with which she resisted the narrowness of the fundamentalist school at which she taught first grade most of her career.

Not until I reached adulthood and after I had expressed my belief that I was called to ministry did she tell me that she had dedicated me in the womb to God and chosen my name (Christopher means "Christ bearer") to reflect that commitment.

Together with my father, Wayne, my mother, Mildred, inspired my faith, along with an appropriate touch of skepticism and doubt—not so much of God, but of all human attempts to capture God. I'm glad they believed in Jesus, but their greater gift to me is that they believed in me, and taught me that God believed in me too.

I dedicated the Lenten portion of this book to my mother on her eighty-third birthday—thus I dedicate this book in her memory. She lived to celebrate her eighty-fourth birthday with the whole family gathered, but unexpectedly joined my father in God's eternal realm a few weeks later. No one will ever love me as long and as well as she did. I am still grieving deeply over this loss, but I am grateful to God for a mother as well as a father who taught me God's love by example, not just in word. Their example continues the reformation of my own heart.

Chris Glaser
Atlanta, Georgia

Using This Book

Both Advent and Lent are "movable feasts." That is, they do not occur on the same dates from year to year. For this reason, their days are not dated, but designated in reference to their numbered weeks on the church calendar. For example, "Tuesday, First Week of Advent" or "Thursday, Third Week of Lent."

Christmas and Epiphany (January 6) are always on the same dates, so Christmastide and the weeks after Epiphany are dated.

During the final week of Advent, please note:

Christmas Eve and Christmas occur on different days after the Fourth Sunday of Advent, depending on the year. The reader is advised to skip to those final meditations on the appropriate days.

During the weeks after Epiphany, please note:

Ash Wednesday, the beginning of Lent, varies, so the reader is advised to skip to the final entry of Epiphany on the Tuesday just before Ash Wednesday, then proceed into the meditations for Lent.

Please note:

Scriptures are from the Inclusive Language Lectionary (based on the Revised Standard Version of the Bible) or the New Revised Standard Version. Occasionally inclusive language changes have been made to the NRSV quotes.

Acknowledgments

There are so many people responsible for whatever inspiration is in these meditations that I could not name them all.
But a few stand out, whose own meditational writings first
gave me the idea of writing meditation books: Malcolm Boyd,
Louis Evely, Michel Quoist, and J. Barrie Shepherd. Since then
I've broadened my meditation horizons, utilizing a broader
spectrum of writers (female and male, people of all colors and
cultures) and writings (not necessarily "spiritual" or "Christian"). All have given me words worthy of shaping my soul.

Of course, my primary text for meditation has always
been the Bible, and I am grateful to biblical characters, writers, translators, interpreters, and scholars whose words
enlighten my mind and enlarge my spirit. My dad liked to
analyze and teach the Bible; my mom liked to read and reflect
on the Bible. Those who read these meditations will recognize both impulses within me.

Half of these meditations are new, but half were published
in earlier forms in prayer books for the *More Light Update*,
the newsletter of More Light Presbyterians. I am grateful to
its editor, James D. Anderson, and the board of what was then
Presbyterians for Lesbian & Gay Concerns, for their encouragement and support in providing devotional material
unique to our community.

I thank my editor, Stephanie Egnotovich, as well as the editorial board and marketing department of Westminster John Knox, for helping to shape the present form of what had been separate sets of meditations. Thanks to Stephanie for making my writing yet more readable, to cover designer Kathy York for rendering an appealing and attractive cover, and to designer Sharon Adams for the overall look and feel of the book. I also wish to thank Ella Brazley for keeping me informed as to the production schedule. Thanks too to all at Westminster John Knox Press responsible for promoting, marketing, and distributing this book and all of my books published by WJK. I gratefully acknowledge bookstore owners who order and sell my books.

I thank those who give this book to others and those who read this book. Until these words are read and heard, they remain idle. Thanks for keeping both me and my words working!

Finally and ultimately, thanks be to God, to Jesus my primary spiritual guide, and to the Spirit who inspires us to look within words for the Word of God.

C.R.G.

PART ONE

Let It Be According to Your Word

*Meditations for Advent
and Christmastide*

Introduction

"Let it be . . . according to your word." With that simple supplication, according to Luke, Mary acknowledged the momentous news the angel Gabriel brought her that she would give birth to one who would be called a child of God.

Thus we begin where the Christian story (and calendar) begins. Those of us trying to reform the church into something more inclusive of lesbian, gay, bisexual, and transgender people have been in labor pains for a quarter of a century, and yet we still keep faith that God is doing a new thing within us and within our spiritual communities. We have faith in God even when our faith in the church is limited.

We say with Mary, the mother of Jesus, "Let it be according to your word," because we believe that God's word will not return to God empty, as the prophet Isaiah declared, "but it shall accomplish that which I purpose, and succeed in the thing for which I sent it" (Isaiah 55:11). The "Word" is God's

---

During the Fourth Week of Advent, please note:
Christmas Eve and Christmas occur on different days of the week after the Fourth Sunday of Advent, depending on the year. Thus, not all of that week's meditations will be used every year. Please skip to Christmas Eve and Christmas Day on the appropriate days.

action in the world. In creation the Word called forth light and life. In the incarnation, that same Word is made flesh, the light and life of humankind (John 1:4).

As Mary did, we have taken that word to heart; we have allowed it to grow within us and given it flesh. Our friends have borne witness to the miracle taking place, and even strangers outside the church have come to marvel at what God is doing through us to liberate the church from legalism, self-righteousness, ignorance, literalism, and the church's resulting despair.

It's been a dirty and earthy business, one that has spoiled our reputation in the eyes of many—so like Mary, unwed mother, who had to account for her sexuality that produced this bastard child whom nobody knew to be God's beloved, mythological afterthoughts of shepherds and Magi notwithstanding. The nativity has been cleaned up, sanitized by the church for its children's pageants, but it was a messy and brutal affair, with Joseph considering abandonment, a barn heaped with manure for the site, a nativity taking place among the poor displaced by bureaucracy and within a country subjugated by a foreign power, an infant barely escaping a leader whose policies led to the death of babies in the ghetto, and a mother with the tenacity to believe in her child all the way to the cross.

However one views the Incarnation, as material or metaphorical truth, it could not have happened without Mary's willing participation. We must be willing, too, to give our bodies in the cause of incarnating God's truth, no matter the rejection, no matter the length of labor, no matter the suffering.

Having begun this Introduction yesterday, last night I had a dream. For the first time in my life, I had a dream I had long coveted, because of its perceived psychological implications of a new beginning. No doubt it was influenced by my contemplation of Mary. I dreamed I was pregnant. Being male, it was, of course, a surprise. But, as dreams go, not that big a surprise in the dream itself. I flashed on the difficulties of pregnancy, of the labor itself. But then I immediately thought of practical concerns—no more wine with dinner, for example. When I awoke, I did not remember the dream until my morning prayers.

In my morning prayers I was reading Gandhi's account of advising an assembly about the nature of taking a vow before God to disobey a civil law in South Africa. It was in his early years in that country that he developed the concept of satyagraha, which literally means "truth" and "firmness," or "truthforce," and, since Gandhi equated truth with love or life's essence, it could be understood as "loveforce" or "soulforce." Gandhi explained that to break a vow was a far greater sin than not living up to an ordinary commitment or promise, because God was invoked as a participant.

The vow that Mary took was that kind of promise: "Here am I, the servant of Adonai; let it be with me according to your word." Though said to Gabriel, angels represented God's presence, so in effect this was her response to God. "Let it be with me according to your word."

For us to echo her words is to take a vow that not even failure or death can break. "Let it be with me according to your word." We too thereby express our intent to allow God's word to become flesh in us.

This has been our call in the service of the welcoming movement, the movement within the church to fully welcome lesbians, gay men, bisexuals, and transgenders (abbreviated herein as LGBT). Together, as the whole church, we are meant to know the truth that has set us all free. Together we are meant to understand that human conditions do not prevent God's word becoming flesh and dwelling in our midst when we are willing to take Mary's vow: "Let it be with me according to your word."

What is that word? It depends on the circumstances into which it is born. Truth. Justice. Mercy. Grace. Love. Joy. Peace. Just as the early church needed the concept of the Trinity to explain its several experiences of God's presence, so we need multiple words to explain God's word to us, in us. But they are all *good* words, because they come from God.

But we need intercourse with the word to render the word flesh. Thus the daily contemplations of this book invite us all to live out Mary's vow: "Let it be with me according to your word." Our call must become our prayer.

Through these Advent and Christmastide meditations, we will contemplate people whose willingness to incarnate God's word made them part of the extended family that produced and inspired Jesus. Matthew's and Luke's genealogies are only part of that story. The spiritual genealogy found in Hebrews 11 of those who lived by faith is also part of Jesus' inheritance, as is the cast of characters in the whole of scripture, including the nativity story. Each day in Advent and Christmastide we will consider how these spiritual ancestors' embodiment of God's word became manifest in Jesus' life and ministry. For example, Jericho's Rahab, a prostitute, a part of Jesus' lineage, led to a Jesus who would defend a woman accused of adultery, allow a "disreputable" woman to wash his feet, and reveal his identity to a Samaritan woman married five times and now living with a man, unmarried. These meditations will not exhaust the list of Jesus' spiritual and genetic family; and Mary, because of her obviously central role, will be the focus of more than one meditation.

> *And Gabriel came to her and said, "Greetings, favored one! The Lord is with you." But she was much perplexed by the angel's words and pondered what sort of greeting this might be.* Luke 1:28–29

We are also startled when told by our "angels" that we are favored and that God is with us. It perplexes us because so many have told us otherwise. We too might be suspicious of this messenger's agenda. Yet this message is central to cultivating an interior life, a life of prayer: to bask in the favor of God's presence.

This may be our unique vocation as lesbian, gay, bisexual, and transgender Christians, and that of our families and friends. Not long ago, reading the writings of women mystics during my own morning prayer, I read what Blessed Elizabeth of the Trinity (1880–1906) posthumously wrote to her own mother superior. I believe it applies to us too. Please hear it addressed to *you*.

> "You are uncommonly loved," loved by that love of preference that the Master had here below for some and which brought them so far. He does not say to you as to Peter: "Do you love Me more than these?" Mother, listen to what He tells you: "*Let* yourself be loved more than these! That is, without fearing that any obstacle will be a hindrance to it, for I am free to pour out My love on whom I wish! '*Let* yourself be loved more than these' is your vocation. It is in being faithful to it that you will make Me happy, for you will magnify the

power of My love. This love can rebuild what you have destroyed. Let yourself be loved more than these." (Quoted in *Prayers of the Women Mystics*, Ronda De Sola Chervin [Charis, 1992], 201–2.)

Our calling may be to bask in God's favor that others do not appreciate. That does not mean others are less loved by God, but we, like Mary, may have the vocation of celebrating God's favor and thereby magnifying the power of God's love for others.

As Mary was startled by Gabriel's message, the Samaritan woman at the well was similarly perplexed by a man, a Jewish rabbi at that, Jesus, speaking to her. "How is it that you, a Jew, ask a drink of me, a woman of Samaria?" she asked (John 4:9). She was unacceptable even among her own scorned race, for she had come alone to collect water in the middle of the day instead of in the morning with the other women of the village, as was the custom of the time. Then Jesus revealed the mysteries of living water, of worshiping in spirit and truth rather than confined by human-made rules and temples, of his being the Messiah. We too are that woman, outcast even from her own people, whom Jesus chooses as an evangelist.

That living water has baptized us and become in us a spring for others, especially other Christians who are dehydrated (and often ossified) by their resistance to God's favor and grace.

Greetings, favored one! The Lord is with you. Let yourself be loved more than these!

> *In the sixth month the angel Gabriel was sent*
> *by God to a town in Galilee called Nazareth, to a*
> *virgin ... [whose] name was Mary.* Luke 1:26–27

Angels are very popular these days, and are no longer confined to either Jewish or Christian mythology. We see their
cherubic faces on stamps, note cards, stickers, refrigerator
magnets, wrapping paper, and so on. People think of them as
pleasant accoutrements to generic spirituality.

But angels must have an edge to them, or Zechariah and
Mary and, later, the shepherds would not have been frightened by their appearance or their words and have needed
comfort, such as "Fear not." They appear in human form, but
scripture hints they do this for our convenience and to avoid
frightening the horses.

Gabriel's name means "hero of God." Earlier he inter-
preted dreams for Daniel, and now announces Jesus' birth. In
addressing Daniel, Gabriel had said, "Daniel, I have now come
out to give you wisdom and understanding. At the beginning
of your supplications a word went out, and I have come to
declare it, for you are greatly beloved. So consider the word
and understand the vision" (Daniel 9:22–23).

Of course I can't resist noting that Gabriel, like us, has
"*come out* to give ... wisdom and understanding." More significantly, Daniel's word of prayer has *called out* that word
which Gabriel has come to declare: the word of Daniel's
belovedness, and a vision of God's word (activity) in the
world. Prayer does that for us too, reminding us of our
belovedness and offering us a vision of things to come, a perspective that places our present troubles in context.

Jesus, too, was ministered to by angels at the end of his sojourn in the wilderness, discerning what it had meant at his baptism to be called "the beloved" and what God wanted him to do. This confirmed his resistance to temptations of survival, reputation, and power, to accept the risk, disrespect, and vulnerability of living on God's word alone, proclaiming a vision of an inclusive spiritual commonwealth.

And throughout his ministry, Jesus frequently sought out a lonely place, a deserted place, to pray. If Jesus needed prayer to keep sight of his value, his vocation, and his vision, how much more do we!

You are greatly beloved. So consider the word and understand the vision.

> *"The Holy Spirit will come upon you, and the*
> *power of the Most High will overshadow you;*
> *therefore the child to be born will be holy."*
> Luke 1:35

If only we had this attitude toward every child born! Yet this very attitude may prompt still more attempts to make a child conform to our expectations and suffer the consequences of nonconformity. I once read of a study that revealed those who "planned" their families were more likely to abuse their children, apparently for not living up to the plan! Transgender children, gay boys, lesbian girls, and bisexual children have not fit "the plan" and have endured the name-calling, ridicule, emotional distancing or downright abandonment, punishment, and abuse given any child who doesn't fit in.

We don't think of the Holy Spirit as being in the baby-making business. The Holy Spirit also must conform to our expectations of what the Spirit is to be and do. The Spirit also suffers abuse for nonconformity. When accused of having a demonic spirit rather than God's Spirit, Jesus snorted, "People will be forgiven for their sins and whatever blasphemies they utter; but whoever blasphemes against the Holy Spirit can never have forgiveness, but is guilty of an eternal sin" (Mark 3:28–29).

Most Christians distrust a Spirit who may blow where it will, as Jesus described it in John 3. "Put a lid on it!" they'd advise charismatic or merely emotional Christians. And to connect that pure Spirit with sex! My God, what are those queer people up to?

But here we have it in Scripture, our sacred text. The Holy Spirit impregnated Mary. Pretty earthy. Certainly the Incarnation further elevates the sanctity of the body, whose nooks and crannies are already shaped by God, first in creation, then in conception ("You knit me together in my mother's womb," Psalm 139:13). God has already connected the Holy Spirit with sexuality.

Of Jesus' forerunner John, an angel said, "Even before his birth he will be filled with the Holy Spirit," and he leapt in the womb at Mary's announcement to Elizabeth. "Now this refutes the Baptists!" Martin Luther might say in defense of infant baptism, according to Luther scholar Roland Bainton.

As we later learn in Acts, neither God nor the Holy Spirit is a respecter of persons, but filled even unbaptized, un-Judaized Gentiles, giving them gifts of the Spirit. It really bugs most Christians that the Spirit has done it again in LGBT people.

But the Spirit bugs us too, as it leads us—as it led Jesus just after his baptism—into a wilderness to be tempted to give up our faith and to renounce our trust in God. No telling what the Spirit is going to do with us and in us. It's downright spooky.

The Holy Spirit will come upon you, and the power of the Most High will overshadow you. What is born in you will be holy.

> *An account of the genealogy of Jesus the Messiah,*
> *the son of David, the son of Abraham.* Matthew 1:1

Before going forward, we must go backward, and look at the family Jesus came from. And his family goes *way* back. (Luke traced it all the way back to Adam and Eve to suggest Jesus' relationship to all peoples, not just Jews.) Abraham was told by God to "Go from your country and your kindred and your father's house to the land that I will show you. I will make of you a great nation, and I will bless you, and make your name great, so that you will be a blessing. . . . In you all the families of the earth shall be blessed" (Genesis 12:1–3). "Abraham believed God, and it was reckoned to him as righteousness," Paul quotes Genesis 15:6 in Romans 4:3.

"Go from your country and your kindred." Jesus proved a chip off this very old block! "Who are my mother and my brothers?" Jesus asked rhetorically. "Whoever does the will of God is my brother and sister and mother" (Mark 3:33, 35). Jesus will make Abraham's family even larger—not by pro-creating, but by extending the family inheritance to others who believe and do the will of God and become part of the family of faith. Thus all the families of the earth shall be blessed by the revelation to the Hebrews of a God of mercy and righteousness.

God's family just keeps getting larger and larger. Luke-Acts traces the Jesus movement from Galilee to Jerusalem, then to the far reaches of the Roman Empire. This new family grew not by ordaining a particular sexual expression, but by inclusiveness. Welcoming Christians are on the same track, proclaiming an inclusive church, anathema to those who promote the "traditional [thus limited and exclusive] family" agenda, but in line with Abraham and Jesus.

"Whoever loves father or mother more than me is not worthy of me; and whoever loves son or daughter more than me is not worthy of me," Jesus reminds the "traditional-family-values" set (Matthew 10:37).

"I will indeed bless you, and I will make your offspring as numerous as the stars of heaven and as the sand that is on the seashore." (Genesis 22:17)

> *"Why did Sarah laugh, and say, 'Shall I indeed bear a child, now that I am old?' Is anything too wonderful for the LORD?"* Genesis 18:13–14

"Nothing will be impossible with God," Gabriel told Mary, announcing the old and "barren" Elizabeth's pregnancy. "Is anything too wonderful for the LORD?" the angel rhetorically asked in the story announcing the nativity of Isaac.

There's a barely perceptible advance between the two stories. Sarah overhears the angel's announcement—hears herself described in the third person as giving birth to a long-promised child. But the angel speaks directly to Mary, and invites her cooperation.

Still, the gist of both stories is that the impossible, the wonderful work of God, cannot be done to us, but with us. In the first, a patriarchal mind-set implies the assent only of Abraham. In the second, God breaks through that mind-set to seek Mary's assent.

Remember when you, like Sarah standing just inside the tent entrance, stood just inside your closet door and perhaps laughed at the possibility that God was going to do something new in you? Is anything too wonderful for the Lord? Nothing will be impossible with God.

Now Christians stand with Sarah just inside the church door, laughing at the thought that God may be doing a new thing in the church, to make it inclusive. Is anything too wonderful for the Lord? Nothing will be impossible with God.

In the context of the seeming impossibility of the salvation of the wealthy, Jesus himself would teach, "For God all things are possible" (Matthew 19:26).

The angels of God are now asking the church in its recent ridicule of the Spirit within us, "Why did you laugh? Is anything too wonderful for the Lord?" And they seek Mary's assent from the church: "Let it be with me according to your word."

Is anything too wonderful for the Lord? Nothing will be impossible with God. Let it be with me according to your word, God. For you all things are possible.

> *Then Abraham reached out his hand and took the knife to kill his son. But the angel of the* Lord *called to him from heaven, and said, "Abraham, Abraham!"* Genesis 22:10–11

This incident must have driven Isaac to a lifetime on a therapist's couch. We can empathize because we may experience our spiritual fathers and mothers in the church ready to sacrifice us metaphorically because they believe it to be God's will. Sometimes our biological fathers and mothers, too.

With Isaac, we remember being a child of promise. Many of us tried hard to be the best little boy or the best little girl in the church family. When our sexuality became known, it was as if our church had this crazy notion that God wanted our removal. We carry within us the psychic scars of this reversal of affection.

We ended up on therapists' couches, joined support groups, and have even done the television talk-show circuit, telling our stories and sharing our pain. The church is just now hearing, "Abraham, Abraham!" When the true will of God finally dawns on the church and it discovers the ram in the thicket, will we be able to forgive its misguided zeal for God, even its misguided love for us?

And will we then stand with the ram in the thicket as Jesus hung with criminals on crosses, declaring that our God is not bloodthirsty, but love-thirsty? Will we join Jesus in saying, "Forgive them, for they know not what they do"? Will we assent to being resurrected, still bearing our wounds, but refusing retribution and reaching for reconciliation, at-one-ment?

Because we have not withheld ourselves, I believe that we will hear God's blessing: "I will indeed bless you, and I will make your offspring as numerous as the stars of heaven and as the sand that is on the seashore. And your offspring shall possess the gate of their enemies, and by your offspring shall all the nations of the earth gain blessing for themselves, because you have obeyed my voice." (Genesis 22:17–18) Mercy begets mercy.

Forgive them, for they know not what they do. But tell them *what they are doing!*

> *Then Judah ... said, "She is more in the right than I."* Genesis 38:26

The first woman mentioned in Matthew's genealogy, Tamar, has a story that is complicated enough for a television mini-series, but which also reads like a daytime soap opera. Her husband, Er, dies and her father-in-law, Judah, follows the law and gives her Er's brother Onan, infamous masturbator or coitus interrupter (depending on your viewpoint), who also dies. Judah resists giving Tamar another son, and sends her away. Later, Tamar allows Judah to think she's a prostitute and gets pregnant by him (send the children to bed now!), later revealing her ploy to obtain justice. Judah recognizes that, by his own legal standards, she is more just.

William Sloane Coffin has said, "The problem is not how to reconcile homosexuality with scriptural passages that appear to condemn it, but rather how to reconcile the rejection and punishment of homosexuals with the love of Christ." If the conservative or even moderate Christians are going to play legalistic games with us, they will find with Judah that we are more in the right than they are. Surely the love of Christ is more difficult to reconcile with their rejection than a paltry few debatable verses (and none from Jesus) with our sexuality.

We must be as clever as Tamar to make this evident to the church.

"Be wise as serpents and innocent as doves," Jesus warned his disciples in facing persecution for proclaiming the gospel (Matthew 10:16).

See, I am sending you out like sheep into the midst of wolves; so be wise as serpents and innocent as doves. Beware of them, for they will hand you over to church councils and flog you in their congregations.

> *"The Holy Spirit will come upon you, and the power of the Most High will overshadow you; therefore the child to be born will be holy; he will be called Child of God."* Luke 1:35

We considered this scripture earlier, when we contemplated the role of the Holy Spirit in the nativity. Now it's time to consider the same passage in reflecting on Mary's role.

Mary was the first charismatic "Christian." She was filled with the Holy Spirit. She did not speak in tongues, she did not preach the gospel, she did not dance in the Spirit. Instead, according to Luke, she paraphrased a prayer that her predecessor Hannah had offered to God when she learned she would give birth to Samuel. And she gave birth to One whose movement would transform the world and, specifically, us.

Last evening, a friend and I rented and watched a video, *The Apostle*, Robert Duvall's homage to "low" Southern evangelical Christianity. Though the protagonist is—to say the least—tarnished, my friend admired the character's absolute faith. The apostle argues with God, sins mightily, and yet boldly proclaims the truth of salvation in a way that common folk can understand. After committing a terrible sin, he baptizes himself in a river and discerns—perhaps egotistically—his calling as an apostle. (As I think of it now, this is not unlike Paul's late-acquired apostleship.)

I recalled how, when I first came to an awareness of my "terrible sin" as a child—that of being homosexual—I fervently attempted an about-face, consciously washing away my sinful identity while taking my daily shower. I prayed for the infusion of the Holy Spirit that would make me like everyone else.

Trouble is, the infusion of the Holy Spirit does just the opposite. Like the charismatic Christians who "annoyingly" raise their hands in praise, or speak a cathartic "gibberish," the Spirit led Mary away from the normal—to conception first and marriage second.

The Spirit has led us too along a path most of us would rather not have taken: being queer in Christ. As with Mary, the Spirit has midwifed in us a movement to recover the innate relationship of sexuality and spirituality, the integral nature of body and spirit, as well as the inclusive nature of the Body of Christ, the church. Just as Mary's conception warranted stoning by the religion of her day, so our conception prompts attacks from the religion of our time. Maybe his mother's vulnerability prompted Jesus to defend the woman from the men accusing her of adultery. May the Body of Christ follow Jesus' lead, defending the vulnerable so violently judged.

Mary, may we, like you, open our wombs to the Holy Spirit, so that the movement that is born of us is vouchsafed sacred.

> *"Surely God is in this place—and I did not know it!"* Genesis 28:16

If Jacob and Esau were gay and lived in Atlanta, Jacob would go to the preppy bar, Blake's, and Esau would go to the leather and bear hangout, The Eagle. I know many of our prejudices in both the straight and gay communities would equate Jacob with gay malehood—you know: gentle, smooth, indoors, a chef, mama's boy, and (loath to admit it) calculating. But Esau fits another stereotype which is gaining ascendancy among gay men: rough, rugged, hairy, outdoors, athletic, a man's man, and (loath to admit it) a little slow on the uptake.

But Jacob made it into Jesus' genealogy by hook and by crook—though, even if Esau could have had such foreknowledge, this would have been the last thing on Esau's mind when it came to being cheated out of the family inheritance and their father Isaac's blessing. As bad as he was, Jacob was nonetheless chosen by God. Escaping Esau's wrath, he came to a place for the night. Not surprisingly, using a rock for a pillow gave him a curious dream that has since given us that song about climbing Jacob's ladder. He woke with the awareness that "Surely the LORD is in this place—and I did not know it!" The rock became the first stone of God's new house.

Later, of course, Jacob would wrestle with God on his way back to reconcile with Esau. To Esau's great credit, the reconciliation was effected.

Seems to me that we are in the place where we play both roles. Cheated out of our inheritance, yet forced to flee. We recognize the presence of God even in the odd places we've slept on the run. We've wrestled with God and received God's blessing. We've faced danger from wrathful siblings, and been willing to reconcile with the ones who stole our inheritance. Like Jacob with Laban, working seven years for Leah and another seven for Rachel, we've worked long and hard for our relationships. Like Esau, we've remained behind to care for aging parents and the family home.

Jesus was in the place where he played both roles too. "Foxes have holes, and birds of the air have nests; but the Human One has nowhere to lay his head" (Luke 9:58). Homeless, yet providing for his mom, even from the cross. Beloved and chosen, yet betrayed and abandoned. Crucified, yet effecting reconciliation. Rejected by religious and political authorities, yet receiving God's blessing and the inheritance of a commonwealth of which he is the firstborn. The rejected stone becomes the cornerstone of God's new home.

Surely our God is in this place—and we did not know it! How awesome is this place! This is none other than the house of God, and this is the gate of heaven. (Genesis 28:16–17)

> *When some Midianite traders passed by, they*
> *drew Joseph up, lifting him out of the pit, and sold*
> *him to the Ishmaelites for twenty pieces of silver.*
> *And they took Joseph to Egypt.* Genesis 37:28

Inflation probably upped the price of betrayal from twenty to thirty pieces of silver by Jesus' time. What siblings did to their brother Joseph, jealous of his dreams and his beloved-ness, a disciple would do to Joseph's descendant Jesus, also envied for his dreams and belovedness.

We can testify that not much has changed. Money has bought our denominations: first, the rich, who will face difficulty getting into the kingdom of heaven because of their enormous financial gifts to reactionary groups in several denominations; second, the wealth of our opposition arrayed against us like the giant Goliath to the boy David; and third, our church siblings so worried about their "bottom line" that we become expendable on the altar of the church's earthly treasures.

Joseph would be put in a place where eventually he would save the very brothers who had betrayed him, saying to them, "Even though you intended to do harm to me, God intended it for good, in order to preserve a numerous people, as God is doing today" (Genesis 50:20). Thus the brothers followed Joseph into Egypt.

Jesus would be put in a place where eventually he would save the very world that crucified him, saying to us, "God did not send the Son into the world to condemn the world, but in order that the world might be saved through him" (John 3:17). Thus we follow Jesus into the commonwealth of God.

In facing our own betrayal at the hands of our brothers and sisters in faith, we have difficulty seeing more light at the end of a very long and very dark tunnel. We fail to see that we are leading them to that light simply by continuing to follow Jesus in the shadows of the church. They are following us following Jesus into more light after all.

Even though they intend harm to me, God intends it for good, in order to preserve my people and all people of faith.

> *Moses brought the people out of the camp to meet God. They took their stand at the foot of the mountain. . . . When the LORD descended upon Mount Sinai, to the top of the mountain, the LORD summoned Moses to the top of the mountain, and Moses went up.* Exodus 19:17, 20

Much, much later, from Mount Nebo and Mount Pisgah, Moses would view the Promised Land that he would not live to enjoy. Given all that he endured, Moses deserved all the mountaintop experiences he was given.

Leadership is tough. People whine. People complain and kvetch. They second-guess and offer hindsight. They pick at your foibles and remember your sins and failures, eternally gossiping about them. They want somebody to do it (often explicit about the "it" that should be done), but won't do it themselves. Good thing Moses had God. As it says at the end of Deuteronomy, "Never since has there arisen a prophet in Israel like Moses, whom the LORD knew face to face" (Deuteronomy 34:10).

Matthew thought Jesus matched Moses, and so placed him on a mount for his famous sermon. But instead of starting with ten commandments, Jesus started with ten beatitudes: "Happy are those . . . ," rather than "Thou shalt not." Jesus called us to live beyond the letter of the law into its spirit of love of God and fellow creatures. In this way we would be blessed. Jesus also seemed to know that the pleasure principle was inspiring and effective in a way that the punitive principle was not.

Luke placed the sermon on a plain, a level place, indicating the egalitarian nature of God's commonwealth. Jesus was the leader, is still the leader, but he calls us all to be leaders. We wanted him to do it all for us—save us, deliver us, take care of us. Such desperate need led to our crucifying this supposed messiah then and repeatedly since. Yet we must "work out [our] own salvation with fear and trembling," as Paul told the Philippians (Philippians 2:12), not without Jesus' help but with his help, not alone but as a community. Together we must discern truth and love and justice. It's a tough job, but somebody's got to do it.

There are those who want to retreat to scripture to determine whether homosexuality is a sin. But the answer lies there no more than in Horatio's stars. The answer lies within the heart of Christ, the Spirit that pulses within us and urges us to let go of our fears and fundamentalism and embrace yet more love.

For it is God who is at work in you, enabling you both to will and to work for God's good pleasure. (Philippians 2:13)

> *"Only Rahab the prostitute and all who are with
> her in her house shall live because she hid the
> messengers we sent."* Joshua 6:17

A prostitute in Jesus' lineage! What will Christians think?

Christians delicately avoid the fact that God works through people that they would not. Indeed, they'd word that last sentence in the past tense: "God *worked* through people that they wouldn't." Surely, they think, God wouldn't do that anymore.

The first gay man I ever met was a male hustler who worked Selma Avenue in Hollywood. In high school, I did not know how to meet other gay people. But I had seen men hanging out on Selma whenever I went into Hollywood for a movie on Hollywood Boulevard, or for pizza at Micelli's on Las Palmas. Selma runs parallel to Hollywood Boulevard, and both streets intersect Las Palmas. (Police harassment moved the hustlers down to Santa Monica Boulevard.) Rumor had it these men were gay, and though the word "hustler" was added to such rumors, I wasn't sure what that meant and, of course, was afraid to ask. I just thought this was how gay men met. I was in for a surprise!

The first gay Christian I ever met was a minister who lived on—guess where?—Las Palmas in Hollywood! That meeting occurred several years after meeting the hustler around the corner. I had read about Bill Johnson's ordination in the newspaper and contacted him, and he invited me to his place for dinner.

The contrast between the visible hustler and the less visible minister serves as a metaphor for any who wish to meet the gay community, either as one trying to affirm one's own homosexuality or as one trying to deny our legitimacy. *Our sexuality may be more apparent than our spirituality.* To discover our spirituality, friend or foe must be welcomed and willing to enter our home and commune with us.

It seems the first resident of Jericho that Joshua's two spies met was the prostitute Rahab. The Bible doesn't say why they were in her house for the night. Suffice it to say that she played a role similar to Lot's in Sodom. She gave the strangers sanctuary, even hid them when the king of Jericho sent orders for her to bring them out, and aided their escape. As a result, she and her family were saved when God destroyed the city, and she was considered a hero in Israelite eyes. If the spies had been afraid of either Rahab's sexuality or their own, they would not have been in a place where God could save all three. Rahab's own faith in their God ("The LORD your God is indeed God in heaven above and on earth below," Joshua 2:11) was thereby revealed.

Jesus must have had an inkling that a prostitute was part of his heritage. Maybe pride in that fact was why he stood in harm's way to protect a woman from being stoned for adultery, defended a woman of ill repute washing his feet, and called to proclaim his gospel a Samaritan woman who had had five husbands and lived with a man, unmarried. Within their sexuality, Jesus saw their faith.

"Listen! I am standing at the door, knocking; if you hear my voice and open the door, I will come in to you and eat with you, and you with me.... Let anyone who has an ear listen to what the Spirit is saying to the churches." (Revelation 3:20, 22)

> *"Do not press me to leave you*
> *or to turn back from following you!*
> *Where you go, I will go;*
> *where you lodge, I will lodge;*
> *your people shall be my people,*
> *and your God my God.*
> *Where you die, I will die—*
> *there will I be buried.*
> *May the* LORD *do thus and so to me,*
> *and more as well,*
> *if even death parts me from you!"*
> Ruth 1:16–17

How well we know this passage! Rarely has the passion of love expressed itself so well. Ruth's love for Naomi surpassed all her other loves—her home, her people, her theology.

There is no doubt that Ruth's blood flowed in Jesus' veins. Even if she were not listed in Matthew's genealogy, we would hear her passion and commitment and tender, loving care in so many of Jesus' sayings and doings:

> "How often have I desired to gather your children together as a hen gathers her brood under her wings, and you were not willing!" (Luke 13:34)
>
> As [Jesus] came near and saw the city, he wept over it. (Luke 19:41)
>
> Jesus . . . was greatly disturbed in spirit and deeply moved. . . . Jesus began to weep. So the Jews said, "See how he loved him!" (John 11:33, 35–36)
>
> "No one has greater love than this, to lay down one's life for one's friends. You are my friends." (John 15:13–14)

"The glory that you have given me I have given them, so that they may be one, as we are one, I in them and you in me, that they may become completely one, so that the world may know that you have sent me and have loved them even as you have loved me." (John 17:22–23)

"And remember, I am with you always, to the end of the age." (Matthew 28:20)

> *As [Hannah] continued praying before the LORD,*
> *Eli observed her mouth. Hannah was praying*
> *silently; only her lips moved, but her voice was*
> *not heard; therefore Eli thought she was drunk.*
> 1 Samuel 1:12–13

Hannah was drunk with devotion to God and a desire for a son. She makes me think of parents who struggle alongside us to obtain full rights for their gay children in the church and in our society. They are drunk with devotion to God and their children.

Our opponents deride them, as the priest Eli derided Hannah, saying, "How long will you make a drunken spectacle of yourself?" (1 Samuel 1:14), adding, "Put away your bias and share our condemnation of your children." Our opponents think themselves like God, able to render justice impartially. But, in truth, our supportive parents are more like God, because God is partial to each and every one of God's children—that's how God shows no partiality. Our supportive parents demonstrate God's steadfast love, and in doing so they demonstrate traditional family values.

In thanksgiving for his birth, Hannah offered her son Samuel to God's service. Her gratitude for her child made her praise and sing to the Lord,

> "My heart exults in the LORD;
>   my strength is exalted in my God.
> My mouth derides my enemies,
>   because I rejoice in my victory. . . .

The bows of the mighty are broken,
    but the feeble gird on strength."
                            (1 Samuel 2:1,4)

Her prayer would serve as model for Mary's own prayer of thanks for a child who would send a Spirit who would make his followers look drunk on the Day of Pentecost. But the inebriation of their fervent devotion to God enabled them to see strangers and aliens as God's children and to speak their language.

Jesus himself was accused of being both glutton and drunkard, because his fervent devotion to God and God's children prompted him to celebrate God's inbreaking commonwealth with those who once thought they were not children of God's household.

"Talk no more so very proudly,
    let not arrogance come from your mouth;
for the LORD is a God of knowledge,
    and by God actions are weighed.
...
God raises up the poor from the dust;
    ...lifts the needy from the ash heap,
to make them sit with rulers
    and inherit a seat of honor."
            (From Hannah's prayer, 1 Samuel 2:3,8)

> *"My soul magnifies the Lord,*
> *and my spirit rejoices in God my Savior,*
> *for God has looked with favor on the lowliness of*
> *this servant.*
> *Surely, from now on all generations will call me*
> *blessed;*
> *for the Mighty One has done great things for me,*
> *and holy is God's name."* Luke 1:46–49

Did Mary really understand the import of her unexpected pregnancy as early as Luke's Gospel indicates? Or was it a gradual dawning insight as she watched Jesus grow "in wisdom and in years, and in divine and human favor" (Luke 2:52)?

It doesn't matter when she "got" it. What matters is she did come to understand the unnatural nature of this son of hers. It's like our baptism, as infants or as adults. It doesn't matter how conscious we were when we were committed to this Jesus—our understanding of that commitment grew through the years. And continues to grow. And it will never be complete until we "know fully, even as [we] have been fully known" (1 Corinthians 13:12).

Jesus' baptism, as well, only initiated his discernment process in the wilderness, tempted in every way as we are.

The same is true of our own movement as lesbians, gay men, bisexuals, and transgenders, our families and friends and advocates—our own nativity of the Spirit. Gradually its long-lasting value will be known. Occasionally, we "get" it, and parallel Mary's prayer as she paralleled Hannah's, as Tony Gryzmala did in an exercise during a Dignity retreat that I led:

My soul magnifies the all-loving God and my spirit rejoices in God my Savior, who esteems, honors, and loves my gayness. Behold, all my family and friends shall recognize my blessedness, for the One who is mighty has done great things for me by creating me in that sacred aspect of the Divine Essence which is gay. Holy is God's name. I praise God and give thanks for being so honored and blest. Through my gayness, God's strength is shown: the proud and the privileged are put down from their thrones; their prerogative is shattered. Through my gayness, God exalts the sensitive, the expansive, the inclusive. God fills my hunger with overwhelming love, while the rich and greedy are sent away in the lonely isolation of their loveless power. Through my gayness, God will heal the human race in remembrance of God's mercy and covenant, as God spoke to Abraham and Sarah, to Noah, to Mary, the Mother of Jesus, and to their posterity forever. Amen.

> *Jesus answered, "Have you not read what David did when he and his companions were hungry? He entered the house of God and took and ate the bread of the Presence, which it is not lawful for any but the priests to eat, and gave some to his companions?"* Luke 6:3–4

David actually negotiated with the priest, who wants to know whether "the vessels of the young men are holy" (see 1 Samuel 21:1–6)! But Jesus uses David's chutzpah to justify his and his disciples' plucking heads of grain to eat on the sabbath, thus breaking the taboo of work on that holy day with slighter justification than, say, healing the man with the withered hand in the story that follows in Luke.

This story makes me think about privilege. Already a hero, David was on his way to snatching the throne. He therefore could easily persuade the priest to bend the Levitical rules to feed himself and his men. Jesus too enjoyed the privilege of success, having developed a following of multitudes and, in the next passage, selecting an executive board (disciples). He could more readily challenge the Mosaic law.

A couple of years ago I wrote a curriculum for a consortium of denominations entitled *Unlearning Racism*. One of the sessions dealt with white privilege; how those of the dominant Anglo-European culture in Canada and the United States could assume things, even "get away with things," that would be questioned if they were persons of color. Another example of this phenomenon is male privilege: men are allowed to do things for which women would be questioned or condemned. Women, too, are allowed to do things for which men would be ridiculed, so there is a certain gender privilege that affects how we may view "effeminate" men or "masculine" women and transgender women and men.

So think about heterosexual privilege: to walk hand in hand, kiss in public, marry, have multiple sexual encounters or failed relationships without being condemned for being heterosexual, adopt children, be included in the family album and gatherings, be welcomed in houses of worship as well as the workplace, and so on.

And, to be both honest and thorough, gay men have some privilege because they're males, and lesbians have some privilege because they're not (that is, it's far less popular culturally to be perceived as giving up one's male privilege to identify as gay).

The "under"privileged had greater difficulty persuading religious leaders to bend Levitical law and move beyond the limits of Mosaic law. But Jesus was the champion of the poor, the disfranchised, the outcast. He could boldly question, "Is it lawful to do good or to do harm on the sabbath, to save life or to destroy it?" (Luke 6:9). It is Jesus, not us, who enjoys the privilege of nudging the church to overlook the law, whether of the Bible or church polity.

So let's introduce the church to Jesus.

Is it lawful to love or to hate gay people, to support same-gender love or destroy it?

TUESDAY, THIRD WEEK OF ADVENT   *BATHSHEBA*

> *So David sent messengers to get [Bathsheba], and*
> *she came to him, and he lay with her.* 2 Samuel 11:4

Now here's an interesting verse to contemplate during Advent!

The much-admired King David had his own White House intern. Except that Bathsheba was married and David's obstruction of justice included the murder of her husband, Uriah. David's independent prosecutor was Nathan, who caught the king in his own judgment and convinced him to say, "I'm sorry."

But what about Bathsheba? Even Matthew's genealogy does not list her by name, but as "the wife of Uriah." Like so many women in the Bible and throughout history, she was acted upon by men, and that served to identify her. "She was asking for it," the sexist might say, bathing where the king could see her. "They were both consenting adults," an audience member on *Oprah* might say, as if she could have said no to a king. Professional boundaries were unknown in that time. Think how biblical the White House has become! And so many pulpits, for that matter! Oh, yes, let's return to *those* traditional family values!

(One might wonder about the parallels to Mary. Could she have said "no" to God? Isn't this a problematic model? That's why taking that story literally does a disservice to God. The story is not about relationships, it is about how Christians perceive Jesus—as a unique Child of God.)

The Bible tells us very little about Bathsheba herself, except that she was "very beautiful" and had the sense to claim David's responsibility by sending him the message, "I am pregnant." She also mourned her husband, Uriah—a sign of faithfulness. And, like many women, she had to suffer the recompense of her then-husband David's sin—by losing her child.

Maybe that's why Jesus spoke so strongly against divorce and adultery. Maybe that's why he addressed women as subjects rather than objects. Maybe that's why he had so many women followers. In his ancestry were stories like this of women treated like property. Jesus proved he was as much a son of Bathsheba as a son of God.

We thank you, God, for the women who have gone before us who have gone unthanked for their unrecognized gifts to the faith we hold so dear.

> *In that region there were shepherds living in the*
> *fields, keeping watch over their flock by night.*
> Luke 2:8

I'm sure none of you had the mischievous thought I had when the media began mentioning that Mother Teresa took her turn cleaning the bathrooms in her order's houses. Wish I got media attention when I scoured my toilet, I thought.

Recently someone called to update me on his current troubles in the church. He spoke reverently of a leader within our community who took time to talk with him at an event, though the leader "despaired" at being besieged by the media. "If the media was there, he probably called them," I wanted to say honestly, knowing this leader's predilection for the press.

Ninety-nine percent of what you and I do does not get our name in the newspapers, will not be recorded, and may even be taken for granted, like the ninety-nine sheep in Jesus' parable who got ignored while that good shepherd searched for that "loose cannon" sheep.

I've come to look on that 99 percent as a spiritual discipline. We don't need spiritual disciplines devised by gurus. If we view fixing meals for a lover or visitor, cleaning the house for the family or guests, earning a living even in a job that isn't quite perfect—if we view these as spiritual opportunities not to think of ourselves more highly than we ought and as forms of service to our loved ones, our customers and clients, our community and God, then these spiritual exercises may also bring us closer to God.

People sometimes recommend monastic communities where I could "get away" and be alone. But the truth is, because I work at home, I *am* alone most of the time. I probably live a more monastic lifestyle than most monks. *My* "retreats" are getting away to be *with* people in my work as a retreat leader. Many of you have a similar experience when you are "alone" in the midst of a busy workplace or an unwelcoming church. These wilderness feelings may also serve as part of our spiritual discipline.

In our ordinary lives as "shepherds," then, we may have a mystical opportunity to listen for God's messengers proclaiming glory and peace, to discern and relish the holy born in our midst.

Jesus washed his disciples' feet long before there were media to flash it around the world. But Jesus *was* savvy enough to know that even the humblest acts reverberate throughout history.

We return to our daily tasks, glorifying and praising God for all we have heard and seen.

> *In the time of King Herod, after Jesus was born in Bethlehem of Judea, wise men [magi] from the East came to Jerusalem, asking, "Where is the child who has been born king of the Jews? For we observed his star at its rising, and have come to pay him homage."* Matthew 2:1-2

Somehow I had missed the connection of the word "magi" and "magic" until a recent PBS documentary on magic mentioned it in the context of what ancient Greeks distrustfully called foreigners with strange religious practices. Later in the program, one of the experts described magic as "ritualized optimism."

I liked that. I believe that our observance of the nativity of Jesus is also a form of ritualized optimism. Many of the stories of Jesus' birth are really stories of how the world *should* have reacted to it. Mary and Joseph should have known of their child's uniqueness before conception, even without the benefit of marriage. Herod should have quaked in his royal boots. Common folk like shepherds should have seen visions of angels. Foreign sorcerers should have recognized the infant's magic.

I believe, however, that the truest story surrounding Jesus' nativity was the poverty and obscurity and homelessness into which he was born, exemplified by there being no room for his parents in the inn, no place for his nativity except a manger in a barn.

It's true that, in our own nativity, when we came out as lesbian or gay or bisexual or transgender, some of us saw stars. Some of us had parents who appreciated our uniqueness.

Our emerging rights aroused fear in those who base their political or religious power on our oppression. Ordinary and extraordinary folk have seen visions of our worth and witnessed our own magic.

But most universal is the poverty and obscurity and homelessness we experienced as we gave up the riches of the closet, risked being forgotten and ignored, and endured exile from all we call home. There is little room in this world for *any* nativity of the Spirit.

And yet there is magic in *every* nativity of the Spirit. Not magic in the sense of manipulation of God, but magic in the sense of God's working within us—our own "ritualized optimism" that all things may work together for good for those who love and trust God.

Jesus was accused of magic, casting out demons by the power of Beelzebub that caused an individual to be mute and visionless (Matthew 12:22–32). Jesus warned of committing the unforgivable sin of misidentifying the Holy Spirit. Even today, our opponents commit that sin, claiming our loss of silence and our gain of vision come from Satan rather than from Jesus.

Baby Jesus, we open our treasure chests and offer you the gifts of our selves, our love, and our homes.

> *"I am Gabriel. I stand in the presence of God, and I have been sent to speak to you and to bring you this good news. But now, because you did not believe my words, which will be fulfilled in their time, you will become mute, unable to speak, until the day these things occur."* Luke 1:19–20

Gabriel is really making the rounds! Getting a little testy, too, because he responds to the "righteous" Zechariah's fear and questions by rendering him unable to speak until the miracle of his wife Elizabeth's pregnancy and the birth of John the Baptist has been accomplished.

If only our opposition, full of fear and questions, were silenced by an angel. Instead, the moderate mainstream remains mute as our opposition bombards us with ridicule, slander, and the removal of privileges and of rights. In my own denomination, the deafening silence was cast as sacred by declaring a "sabbatical" on our welcome! In other words, neither side was to push the issue.

Such an attempt to Christianize wimping out on our rights in both the church and society is laughable when one thinks of Jesus' attitude toward the sabbath (from which *sabbatical* derives). The sabbath was made for us, not us for the sabbath, he declared over and over again, proving it by healing on the sabbath at the drop of a hat, feeding his disciples on that sacred day, and stirring up controversy on that day of rest.

Those on Jesus' side will continue to heal on the sabbath instead of using it as an excuse to allow lesbians, gays, bisexuals, and transgenders to be spiritually abused by those who temporarily have the upper hand in the church.

Immediately [Zechariah's] mouth was opened and his tongue freed, and he began to speak, praising God. Fear came over all their neighbors. (Luke 1:64–65)

SATURDAY, THIRD WEEK OF ADVENT   *ELIZABETH*

> *After those days his wife Elizabeth conceived. . . .*
> *She said, "This is what the Lord has done for me*
> *when [God] looked favorably on me and took*
> *away the disgrace I have endured among my*
> *people."* Luke 1:24–25

It's a shame that the goal of sexuality came to be procreation.
The same type of people who abused Elizabeth for not having children are the ones who, today, abuse those of us whose
sexuality does not produce children.

Luke tells us that Elizabeth and Zechariah both lived
"blamelessly according to all the commandments and regula-
tions of the Lord" (Luke 1:6). But no matter how squeaky-clean
their lifestyle, the fact that they hadn't produced children
meant *she* was blamed, disgraced, and ridiculed, much like
Hannah before the birth of Samuel. Beyond the gender
inequity of such condemnation, what about the inequity
between the haves and have-nots, between those who had
children and those who didn't?

Seems as if the spiritual community should have a different standard than the mere biological requirement of repro-
duction. Seems as if the community concerned with the
sacred would recognize the holy in sexuality apart from any
product.

That's the kind of spiritual community Jesus wanted.
That's why he defended the eunuch as Isaiah did. That's why
members of the new spiritual community would be called
his brothers and sisters. That's why our own spiritual communities have to get over themselves and recognize us as
siblings.

This is what the Lord has done for us when God looked favorably on us and took away the disgrace we have endured within the church.

> *"[God] has scattered the proud in the imagina-*
> *tion of their hearts."* Luke 1:51 (RSV)

In truth, God does not really need to step in to scatter
the proud. The "imagination of their hearts" is quite enough
for the proud, the arrogant, to mistake their connection
with the humble, the outcast. Maybe the proud are not altogether bad people, but they have bad or at least inadequate
imaginations.

Mary had a good imagination, one capable of wrapping
itself around the plausibility of God's becoming a vulnerable
human being, of humbly entering human history, and forever
changing, if not the whole world, a good portion of it. If God
can do it, the high and mighty can, and so the powerful
are brought down from their thrones, the rich sent away
empty—unless they realize that their real wealth is to be
found in solidarity with others: the vulnerable, the poor.

"The Spirit of the Lord is upon me"—Jesus claimed for
himself Isaiah's prophecy—

> "because [God] has anointed me
>   to bring good news to the poor.
> [God] has sent me to proclaim release to the captives
>   and recovery of sight to the blind,
>   to let the oppressed go free,
> to proclaim the year of the Lord's favor."
>
> (Luke 4:18–19)

Jesus also had an excellent imagination.

Advent is a time to practice our imagination, to press our

credulity to the limits, as we await the entrance of God into our world.

"It is easier for a camel to go through the eye of a needle than for someone who is rich to enter the kingdom of God," Jesus told his disciples (Mark 10:25)—those rich not only in possessions, I imagine, but in "righteousness" as well. They too would have to give up all their possessions, their good deeds, their obedience to the law, to come unburdened into the commonwealth of God.

We must imagine, we must hope, that because "for God all things are possible" (Mark 10:27), even our opponents will let go of their heterosexrighteousness (yes, my own word) to sit at table with us in the commonwealth of God.

Surely, from now on all generations will call us blessed: for the Mighty One has done great things for us, and holy is God's name. (Luke 1:48–49)

_____

Because Christmas occurs on different days of the following week in different years, skip to Christmas Eve and Christmas on the appropriate days.

"Joseph, son of David, do not be afraid to take Mary as your wife, for the child conceived in her is from the Holy Spirit. She will bear a son, and you are to name him Jesus, for he will save his people from their sins." Matthew 1:20–21

Spoken by another angel, written in another Gospel. Luke left it to Matthew to explain Joseph's cooperation in the whole affair, a dream in which an angel spoke the words above. Joseph had another dream that warned the family to flee the impending massacre of the innocents to Egypt, and yet another dream informed him that Herod was dead and the family could return to Israel. Still one more dream told him to move into Galilee, specifically Nazareth.

Like his namesake ancestor, this Joseph was also a dreamer. His dreams saved Mary from disgrace, the baby Jesus from death, and the whole family from remaining refugees, and fulfilled the prophecy that "He will be called a Nazorean" (Matthew 2:23).

But, other than that, the Bible doesn't tell us much about him, except that father and son were carpenters, and that Joseph and Mary went on to have other children, apparently all by themselves.

Yet maybe it was from his foster dad that Jesus got the idea of likening the one who truly listened to his words to one who wisely constructed a house on rock rather than sand, or likening discipleship to the commitment of the builder of a tower who figures out the cost before proceeding with the foundation.

Or maybe, and more importantly, beneath such solid construction stories, Jesus received from Joseph a foundation in dreams. Maybe Joseph's dreams led to Jesus' dreams of saving outcasts from disgrace, delivering everyone from the bondage to law and sin and death, calling us home to God, and claiming our destiny as children of God.

When Joseph awoke from sleep, he did as the angel of the Lord commanded him (Matthew 1:24). *As we awake, may we too follow our God-given dreams.*

> *"This child is destined for the falling and the rising of many in Israel, and to be a sign that will be opposed so that the inner thoughts of many will be revealed—and a sword will pierce your own soul too."* Luke 2:34-35

Simeon is usually remembered for his Nunc Dimittis, which he proclaimed loudly and poetically in the temple while holding the baby Jesus. But this somewhat more cryptic remark Simeon addresses to Mary very personally. Mary will suffer with her son, Jesus, for the sins of the world.

Mothers reading this know that such suffering is often more difficult to bear than being the direct recipient of pain. Observers see it on television in the anguish of a mother whose child has become a victim of gun violence, spineless legislators for sale, and a gun lobby that's as irrational as any lunatic on a shooting spree. Observers may also see it in their church in the tears of a mother whose child has become the victim of spiritual violence, an ignorant and cowardly denomination, and reactionary groups in our churches that are as rabid as any gay basher.

The child will "be a sign that will be opposed so that the inner thoughts of many will be revealed." Children often serve as a kind of Rorschach test for adults. If you ever want to find out an adult's true nature, just discreetly watch what they do when they unexpectedly encounter a child.

Jesus admonished the disciples for resisting children who wanted to come sit on Uncle Jesus' lap. And, in another circumstance, he confirmed what Simeon had foretold about the revelation of the opposition's inner thoughts: "So have no fear of them; for nothing is covered up that will not . . . become known" (Matthew 10:26).

Our own opposition's agenda will be made known: their desire to take over our denominations, make them over into their reactionary image, and promote the evil spirit of antichrist, which opposes all that Jesus stood for when he said of the children of God, young and old, "Let the little children come to me" (Luke 18:16) and "Whoever welcomes this child in my name welcomes me" (Luke 9:48). Our opposition are the modern-day scribes and Pharisees who "cross sea and land to make a single convert, and . . . make the new convert twice as much a child of hell as [them]selves" (Matthew 23:15).

The baby Jesus reminds us to end the murder of the innocents at the hands of the self-righteous hungry for power and control, whether in the courts of the land or in the courts of the church.

"My eyes have seen your salvation, which you have prepared in the presence of all peoples." (Luke 2:30–31)

> *At that moment [Anna] came, and began to praise God and to speak about the child to all who were looking for the redemption of Jerusalem.* Luke 2:38

Luke was the first evangelist to use inclusive language. He included stories about women, Samaritans, and Gentiles, whose faith Jesus praised, and to whom he offered healing and revealed spiritual truth. Not surprisingly, Luke balances the story of Simeon with the story of Anna, eighty-four years old, who "never left the temple but worshiped there with fasting and prayer night and day" (Luke 2:37). We don't have a quote from her, but at least we have the story.

Anna is the sort of woman "of great age" (Luke 2:36) that I see in our church on Sunday, that you probably see in your church too. The women who welcome me do not care about my sexuality—they care about me and about my relationships with people. They say and demonstrate how pleased they are that I am there. Their smiles are genuine. Their concern over recent church votes against my kind shows in their faces when the congregation discusses these matters.

Jesus saw their faith and welcome in his day too: the woman who touched the hem of his garment, the woman bent over by unseen burdens for many long years, the woman who put everything she had into the Temple treasury, the women who beat their breasts and wailed for him on his way to the cross, the women who stood at the foot of his cross, and the women who rejoiced at his resurrection.

Though not in my congregation, I suppose there are

elderly women who oppose gay people's having rights and privileges. But I am convinced that if our denomination were made up of women of great age, gays and lesbians would have been ordained long ago.

Perhaps God could not reveal God's self in female form at the time of Jesus, but now I see God in the glowing faces of faithful old women. And I praise God and write about them to all who are looking for the redemption of the church.

We praise you, God, for those in our congregations whose welcome counterbalances the recent unpleasantness of church votes against us.

> *"Bring my sons from far away*
> *and my daughters from the end of the earth—*
> *everyone who is called by my name,*
> *whom I created for my glory,*
> *whom I formed and made."*
> *Bring forth the people who are blind, yet have eyes,*
> *who are deaf, yet have ears! ...*
> *You are my witnesses, says the LORD.* Isaiah 43:6–8, 10

The book of Isaiah declares that those with disabilities may have the insight and the discernment to recognize the new thing God does for God's people. Along with so many other nontraditional members of the faith community described in Isaiah, they would serve as witnesses of what they have "seen" and "heard" of God's glory. Remember, the visually and hearing impaired could not be ordained as priests, according to the Law of Moses.

In spirit at least, Isaiah and his school of disciples would be in sync with Unitarian Universalists when they wrote, "Before me no god was formed, / nor shall there be any after me," quoting God in the same breath as our text (Isaiah 43:10). And God's "house shall be called a house of prayer / for all peoples" (Isaiah 56:7), including religious outcasts, Isaiah declares, striking a universalist theme.

Isaiah's calling would serve as text for Jesus' own calling (Luke 4:18–19), and his book's Suffering Servant passages would be applied to Jesus by early Christians. Isaiah and his disciples, who wrote the prophetic insights we read in the book given Isaiah's name, were surely the spiritual progenitors of Jesus.

Just as we believe God's Word was made flesh in Jesus, so Isaiah's words are made flesh in Jesus' ministry. The man born blind, found in the ninth chapter of John's Gospel, was considered a sinner in the eyes of the Pharisees. Even the disciples asked Jesus whether sin caused his disability. Jesus corrected: "He was born blind so that God's works might be revealed in him" (John 9:3).

The man born blind became a witness to God's glory manifest in Jesus, saying to religious leaders, "He is a prophet" (9:17), and, "If this man were not from God, he could do nothing." The Pharisees responded, "We know that God has spoken to Moses, but as for this man, we do not know where he comes from." Jesus would later comment to the effect that their certainty of their ability to see blinded them to a new reality (9:41).

Our community bears witness to God's glory that we witness in our sexualities and our gender identities. We are dismissed as sinners only because contemporary Pharisees allow their certainty to blind them to new realities.

Just as the blind see things differently and the deaf hear things unsaid, we feel things differently and know different realities. Open all people of faith to our witness, O God, and open us to the witness of those different from ourselves.

> *The wolf shall live with the lamb,*
> *the leopard shall lie down with the kid,*
> *the calf and the lion and the fatling together,*
> *and a little child shall lead them.*
> Isaiah 11:6

Anticipating the difference the Messiah would make to all of creation, Isaiah imagined a world of harmony even among animals. Luke 2:7 describes Jesus being placed in a manger, a feeding trough for animals. Traditional depictions of the scene show animals gathered around Mary, Joseph, and the newborn Jesus.

Jesus' ministry began in rural Galilee. His illustrations of God's care and commonwealth were filled with references to animals and plants: the birds of the air, the lilies of the field, the sparrow fallen to the ground, the weeds in the harvest, the mustard seed, foxes and their lairs, a sheep fallen in a pit, the lost lamb, the sowing of seeds, himself as mother hen, and so on. Jesus cared not only for the human "least of these"—from the moment of birth, animals played a role in Jesus' ministry and message.

I learned that the Atlanta Humane Society, from which I had adopted my dog, was originally formed to protect the rights of women and children as well as animals! It came as a surprise to me, but on reflection, one can see the necessity, given the vulnerability of all three categories. Women, children, and animals frequently have suffered abuse, exploitation, and all manner of inhumane treatment.

Jesus defended women in his ministry, welcomed the

little children to come unto him, and knew that animals reveal God's care for all of us, as well as offer insights into the nature of all things.

God of all creatures, free us from our human narcissism and narrow-mindedness so that we may see your beauty, your care, your holiness, and your blessing in every creature.

> *When Elizabeth heard Mary's greeting, the child*
> [John] *leaped in her womb.* Luke 1:41

Now this was a precocious child: already filled with the Holy Spirit, already aware of Jesus' uniqueness. "Blessed are those who have not seen and yet have come to believe," Jesus would say (John 20:29). Though presented as kin by Luke, other Gospels testify that they meet each other for the first time at the River Jordan, where John is a voice crying in the wilderness. Even in Luke it's not clear they already know each other.

Nothing about John's lifestyle would get him called "a glutton and a drunkard," as Jesus would be accused. His renunciation of a comfortable life gave him the authority to call others to repentance. We all know of people like this who work with the homeless, the hungry, prisoners, death-row inmates, the sick, the disfranchised, minorities, victims and causes of war, the poor, the abused, people with mental disabilities, those with physical disabilities, the dying. Those who do such work are truly voices crying in the wilderness, and they are disturbing to be around. Their austerity, their asceticism, call us to reexamine our own excesses, to repent or at least redirect whatever resources we have, whether of time, or money, or compassion.

Even Jesus was called to be baptized by John. John served as Jesus' guidepost to the wilderness and to the promised kingdom, or commonwealth, beyond. If even a Messiah like Jesus needed spiritual direction, how much more do we!

"Prepare the way of the Lord." . . . *"Whoever has two coats must share with anyone who has none; and whoever has food must do likewise."* (Luke 3:4,11)

> *And [Mary] gave birth to her firstborn son and*
> *wrapped him in bands of cloth, and laid him in*
> *a manger, because there was no place for them in*
> *the inn.* Luke 2:7

Despite so rich an inheritance in terms of genealogy as well as spiritual ancestry and community, Jesus' beginning was less auspicious than most of our own births. Is this the way God chooses to enter the world, and our own lives as well? Through the back door, unnoticed, ignored, and so vulnerable?

As if to correct this oversight, the angels got together and sang a cantata in the heavens. But to whom? Shepherds?! Were they so unsavvy mediawise? Better to announce the birth to celebrities, or to Rome, or at least in the urban center of Jerusalem, not off on some lonely hilltop to a bunch of hillbillies.

And whose idea was the star? Attracting foreign scholars whose religion is suspect to worship the king of the Jews? How will that help his credibility among his own people?

Whoever imagined that God could come into the world as an infant? Wait till the traditionalists get hold of *this* reimagining of God! They'll decry illiterate shepherds' speaking out of personal experience rather than the Torah, and ridicule the scholars who testify to Jesus' spiritual worth.

The Temple, or headquarters, of each and every one of our denominations will quake in its foundations, for, having just avoided trouble by scapegoating gays and lesbians, now they will have to figure out a way to deal with this newest nativity of the Spirit.

How heretical to conceive of God as a baby reaching out for our love! How scandalous to think of God embodied in human flesh! How impure to believe God would reach out to touch the unclean! How absurd to understand God offering God's self for our salvation! How unorthodox to affirm that God's Word could become flesh!

"I am the living bread that came down from heaven. Whoever eats of this bread will live forever; and the bread that I will give for the life of the world is my flesh." . . . [Jesus] said these things while he was teaching in the synagogue at Capernaum.

When many of his disciples heard it, they said, "This teaching is difficult; who can accept it?" But Jesus, being aware that his disciples were complaining about it, said to them, "Does this offend you?" . . .

Because of this many of his disciples turned back and no longer went about with him. (John 6:51, 59–61, 66)

God's Word became flesh so that Jesus may serve as bread for us, so that God's Word in Jesus may be transformed to flesh within us as the Body of Christ. As that Body, we reach out for love and in love, we touch the unclean and embrace the outcast, we offer ourselves for the transformation of the world in unorthodox ways. God's Word will not return to God empty, but will accomplish what God intended: Truth. Justice. Mercy. Grace. Love. Joy. Peace.

Let it be with me according to your Word, O God!

> *In those days a decree went out from Emperor Augustus that all the world should be registered. . . . All went to their own towns to be registered. Joseph also went from the town of Nazareth in Galilee to Judea, to the city of David called Bethlehem, because he was descended from the house and family of David. He went to be registered with Mary, to whom he was engaged and who was expecting a child.* Luke 2:1, 3–5

And that's how Jesus came to be born in Bethlehem.

As much as we might enjoy "a nice little Christmas" without politics, the very place of Jesus' birth was determined, however inadvertently, by the politician Emperor Augustus and by an imperialist power, Rome.

Our place in the church and in society has also been determined by politics. Though we might wish for a spirituality that somehow "rises above politics," there ain't no such thing! There's politics within the church, and outside politics affects the church. Major bucks are coming from secular reactionary foundations and organizations to scare the church to the right as one more front in their declared "culture wars"—a term coined in Nazi Germany.

Getting warm and fuzzy feelings and singing "Kum ba Yah" with our adversaries will not make our divisions disappear. Christians caught in the middle might be persuaded that "both" sides have been hurt in the struggle for our equal rights, but when all is said and done, *we're* the ones without rights: civil rights and church rights. And we're *not* the ones demanding the other side's rights be denied.

"Is it lawful to pay taxes to the emperor, or not?" Pharisees once asked Jesus, hoping to trap him (Matthew 22:15–22). Jesus asked to see the coin needed to pay the tax, a coin that had the emperor's likeness on it. He held it up and said, "Give . . . to the emperor the things that are the emperor's, and to God the things that are God's."

Joseph and Mary went to Bethlehem to be registered, as demanded by the emperor. But they gave birth to One who would cunningly put the emperor in his place: under God, the higher authority. We can do no less. We must put the pope and the president and the prime minister and all priests and ministers in their places *under* God.

All authority outside of yours, God, is secondhand. Help me to always give you your due, far above any worldly or churchly authority.

> *When Herod saw that he had been tricked by the*
> *wise men, he was infuriated, and he sent and*
> *killed all the children in and around Bethlehem*
> *who were two years old or under.* Matthew 2:16

Providentially, Joseph had been warned in a dream to take Mary and the baby Jesus away before the carnage. The Magi themselves had been warned in a dream not to return to Herod and give up the whereabouts of the baby they had sought as king of the Jews.

Every drama needs a bad guy, a villain we can hiss! There always seem to be some reactionaries around when something good happens. Envy, fear, loathing, ignorance, prejudice, cowardice, inequity, injustice are all unveiled in the hearts of those who wish to thwart any nativity of God's Spirit in our midst, even if the form is only that of an innocent, vulnerable baby.

Herod was a Jewish puppet of the Roman oppressors, set up as a local king to give some semblance of self-rule. He wanted no competition for the throne, either his throne or that of his children. He later imprisoned John the Baptist for criticizing him for taking his brother's wife, and, albeit reluctantly, served up John's head on a platter (Mark 6:17–29).

We might think of Christian puppets, ranging from local pastors to church bureaucrats, who care more about their positions than our position. We might think of gay puppets, ranging from so-called ex-gays to closeted, homophobic homosexual leaders in the church and culture, whose self-loathing gets projected onto us.

The church and culture have villainized *us*, and sometimes we too forget that we have innocently come into our self-awareness, humbly and vulnerably offering ourselves, our gifts, and our relationships to our churches, our nations, our cultures.

"Let the little children come to me; do not stop them; for it is to such as these that the kingdom of God belongs," Jesus said in defending the innocent and vulnerable. Moreover, he suggested that innocence and vulnerability are the qualities required for the nativity of God's commonwealth: "Whoever does not receive the kingdom of God as a little child will never enter it." (See Mark 10:13–15.)

In the face of those who allege our guilt before God and our unwarranted political power, Jesus, take us in your arms, reminding us of our innocence and our vulnerability. Lay your hands upon us, blessing us.

> *Then the prophet Miriam, Aaron's sister, took a*
> *tambourine in her hand; and all the women*
> *went out after her with tambourines and with*
> *dancing. And Miriam sang to them, "Sing to the*
> *LORD, for God has triumphed gloriously."* Exodus
> 15:20–21

Thus the children of Israel celebrated the defeat of the Egyptians and the end of their enslavement and oppression. Early Christians would draw parallels between that redemption of God's children, the Hebrews, and the redemption of God's children in Jesus Christ. We were now freed *from* the overreaching of the law, the burden of sin, and the concept that death ends everything. We were freed *for* grace, forgiveness, and abundant life.

When I had my first contact with another gay Christian, a gay Christian minister named Bill Johnson, I put on the Broadway musical album *Jesus Christ Superstar* and danced for joy, all by myself. We had only made arrangements over the phone to meet the next evening for dinner, but already I knew freedom was on its way. I experienced joyful ecstasy.

Of course trouble lay ahead, too. But the glory of knowing there was someone else out there like me—gay, Christian, wanting to serve in ministry—was a transforming experience. Even that sells the event short. It was *metanoia*. I would never be the same, *thank God!*

"But to what will I compare this generation? It is like children sitting in the marketplaces and calling to one another, 'We played the flute for you, and you did not dance.'"
Jesus said this, contrasting his own celebrative ministry with

the somber ministry of John the Baptist. Some claimed John had a demon, because of his ascetic ways. But now the same folk complained of Jesus, "Look, a glutton and a drunkard, a friend of tax collectors and sinners!" (See Matthew 11:16-19.)

The closet was a place of penance and prayer. Coming out is a sacrament for singing and celebration. Let's dance!

Flute Player, may I give myself over to the ecstasy of your dance of freedom! Hallelujah! Amen!

> *After three days they found him in the temple....*
> *His mother said to him, "Child, why have you*
> *treated us like this?"...He said to them, "Why were*
> *you searching for me? Did you not know that I*
> *must be in my Father's house?"...His mother trea-*
> *sured all these things in her heart.* Luke 2:46,
> 48–49, 51

A recent film tells the story of Jesus from Mary's point of view. Appropriately, the movie indicates how a mother's influence may have shaped his own teachings. Though our patriarchal world recognizes mostly men and most often records *their* words and acts, the truth of the matter is that these men were taught, inspired, and influenced by mothers, sisters, aunts, daughters, grandmothers, and granddaughters. It must have been so with Jesus.

How tender the sentence, "His mother treasured all these things in her heart."

Most of our mothers who became supportive of us treasured early insights into our personalities as well, discerning who we were and who we were called to be. They may have been "amazed" and "astonished" as Jesus' parents were, and they may have reproached us as well, not fully understanding where God called us to be.

The film suggests Mary's hurt when she comes to visit Jesus and he replies, "Whoever does the will of God is my brother and sister and mother" (Mark 3:35). Yet the one who viewed the faithful as family nonetheless provided for his mother from the cross, saying to the beloved disciple, "Here is your mother," and to his mother, "Woman, here is your son" (John 19:26–27).

Many of our mothers and fathers have stood with Mary beside the crosses of daughters and sons who agonized over their sexuality, suffered rejection and excommunication, and possibly endured an otherwise forsaken death, whether of suicide, addiction, AIDS, or cancer. All such parents are part of our family, because "Whoever does the will of God is our brother and sister and mother."

We are family! Thank you, Mary, for setting the example for your son Jesus and for us.

> *The first man was from the earth, a man of dust;*
> *the second man is from heaven....Just as we have*
> *borne the image of the man of dust, we will also*
> *bear the image of the man of heaven.* 1 Corinthi-
> ans 15:47, 49

Matthew's genealogy of Jesus begins with Abraham, but Luke's, in reverse order, ends with Adam, "son of God" (Luke 3:38). In his Gospel, Luke repeatedly found ways to proclaim that Jesus is for everybody. While Matthew wanted to demonstrate Jesus' Jewish identity, Luke revealed Jesus as related to every human being, descendant of the first couple.

In Corinthians, the apostle Paul compares the first Adam to Jesus, the "last Adam." Paul uses this comparison to explain the physical and spiritual dimensions of human experience. In Romans, Paul uses the contrast to claim that death came into the world through Adam and his sin, while life came to everyone through Jesus and God's grace. Adam's behavior required the law, while Jesus's life, death, and resurrection offered us forgiveness, justification, and eternal life. (See Romans 5:6–21.)

So, to reframe the feminist bumper-sticker message, "Adam *was* a rough draft." Jesus lived the way human beings were intended to live. Yet Jesus was very much the son of Adam, so the spiritual life—and heaven itself—is not unreachable by other human beings.

Jesus made the spiritual life accessible to mere mortals. He criticized the religious leaders of his day, saying, "For you load people with burdens hard to bear, and you yourselves do not lift a finger to ease them" (Luke 11:46). Think of the celibacy required of gays and lesbians to be considered moral or to be ordained. And in Matthew's version of this saying, it is implied that religious leaders do not share burdens they place on others (Matthew 23:3–4). What church requires celibacy of all of its heterosexual members?

Many if not most of us growing up aware that we were different tried to be the "best little boys and girls," perfect in every way but one. But, for the sake of our spiritual health, we had to let go of perfectionism to discover integrity. That's exactly what Jesus called for in all people, especially the hypocrites criticized in Luke 11 and Matthew 23.

"Come to me, all you that are weary and are carrying heavy burdens, and I will give you rest. Take my yoke upon you, and learn from me; for I am gentle and humble in heart, and you will find rest for your souls. For my yoke is easy, and my burden is light," Jesus said (Matthew 11:28–30).

Lighten my spirit, Jesus, yearning for you, that I may fly.

> *I permit no woman to teach or to have authority over a man; she is to keep silent. For Adam was formed first, then Eve; and Adam was not deceived, but the woman was deceived and became a transgressor.* 1 Timothy 2:12–14

Well, actually, the story goes that the man was also deceived! And we were reminded yesterday that Adam was the rough draft of human beings. The late gay scholar John Boswell liked to point out that the whole creation story led to higher forms of life day by day, and woman was the last form of life created in a clearly ascending hierarchy!

Poor Eve! She had never been lied to before and had neither inborn nor learned discernment of right and wrong when she listened to the serpent about the tree of the knowledge of good and evil. As a result women were given the pain of childbirth in the Genesis story; in Timothy, women "will be saved through childbearing" and must be submissive to their husbands.

In our innocence, we too listened to "serpents" tempting us spiritually and sexually. We have had to learn on our own—sometimes as a community, sometimes as individuals—which of our behaviors chooses life, offers love, and serves others best. Sexuality itself has been viewed as being "saved" or redeemed by procreation, while we have affirmed sexuality as itself redemptive, calling us to ourselves and into relationships, giving us occasions to praise and thank God. We have been commanded to submission by the dominant heterosexual culture, because we were not in the Garden of Eden. Yet, if one takes the story literally, one has to admit that it was through heterosexuals that sin came into the world.

Jesus, however, knew that men were pigs (smile). That's why he defended women of his day. In one particular reference (Matthew 19:3–12), he may be viewed by some as defending marriage. But, in truth, since it was women who suffered in divorces of his time, he was more likely defending women. And in that context he surprisingly defended "eunuchs," those who could not or chose not to procreate. Jesus also included women among the broader circle of his disciples, and eunuchs were included in the early church (Acts 8:26–40).

Eve was so named because in Hebrew her name looks like *living*, and "she was the mother of all living" (Genesis 3:20). As we "live it up" tonight on New Year's Eve, making New Year's resolutions for bettering our "living," let's remember mother Eve, who gave us fruit from the tree that could help us discern good from evil. And with her descendant Jesus' guidance, let's choose the good.

Eve, mother of all human beings who have lived and are living, thank you!

> *Adam knew his wife again, and she bore a son
> and named him Seth, for she said, "God has
> appointed for me another child instead of Abel,
> because Cain killed him."* Genesis 4:25

Seth, like this day, is a new beginning. He is the Abel replacement
and apparent counter to Cain, who has taken to building cities
in Genesis 4:17 after murdering his brother in Genesis 4:8.
Things moved fast back then; after all, there was a lot of ground
to cover. Cain's near descendants began to specialize: one
became "the ancestor of those who live in tents and have live-
stock," another was "the ancestor of all those who play the lyre
and pipe," and still another "made all kinds of bronze and iron
tools." And we thought it took ages to accomplish all this stuff!
Of course, they were living for hundreds of years in those days!

   Just as in the stories of today, the bad guys like Cain are always
more intriguing and get more coverage than the good guys. The
Bible doesn't tell us much about Seth, other than listing him in
genealogies in Genesis, 1 Chronicles, and the one we have from
Luke. Because a murderer began urban sprawl, Seth may very
well have occupied Abel's place as a shepherd in rural areas.

   Jesus was one of the rare good guys who got a lot of attention. He began his ministry in the rural region of Galilee, and his
parables and metaphors were rural in nature. The lilies of the
field, the birds of the air, the vineyard, the fig tree, the sower, the
weeds in the wheat, the treasure in the field, fishers of men and
women, the lost sheep, the farmer's prodigal son—all rural
images that made his message memorable, even if his listeners
didn't always "get it" at first hearing.

   He took his message to the city, Jerusalem, and it got him

killed. What do you expect? The first city was founded by Cain. Even as Jesus cried over the city, he yearned to gather it together "as a hen gathers her brood under her wings" (Luke 13:34).

We who have been deemed "*un*natural" by the church have often retreated to nature for God's solace, ranging from our pets and gardening to living or vacationing in rural areas and natural settings. In those moments, in those places, God's earth heals our earth. And in harried city life, Jesus' rural images may serve as icons of tranquillity and redemption.

Touch me with the redemptive earth that brought vision to the one born blind, growth to the well-planted seed, and plentiful harvest to those who are aware.

Now the earth was corrupt in God's sight, and the earth was filled with violence....And God said to Noah, "I have determined to make an end of all flesh, for the earth is filled with violence because of them; now I am going to destroy them along with the earth. Make yourself an ark." Genesis 6:11, 13–14

We're all grateful that God doesn't continue using this remedy to corruption and violence, else we'd all be building arks. "But Noah found favor in the sight of the LORD" because he was a "righteous man" (Genesis 6:8–9), so God decided Noah and his family would be saved to repopulate the earth, along with two of every species of animal. After it was all over, God would lay down a colorful bow in the heavens as a sign of the new covenant with humankind never to destroy the earth this way again.

This is a harsh God. But they were harsh times, and good people imagined a god that would respond in the same way *they* would—unmercifully. But I wonder if God was framed by our projections of what deity is all about. I wonder if God hasn't always had to shake God's self loose from all our vain imaginings of who God is or how God acts, especially in history. Surely God shuddered (and shudders) at all our "holy" wars, our violent crusades against "infidels" and other queers, our inquisitions, witch hunts, and excommunications.

Jesus put a different face on God, as a devoted friend willing to give his life for us. His God was the good shepherd willing to search for the lost sheep, the father eagerly waiting for the return of his prodigal son, the mother hen seeking to shelter her brood. Yet Jesus also warned of being prepared for the day when "the Son of Man" would come to earth, contrasting his ancestor Noah with the people of his time who lived life without regard to God (Luke 17:26-27).

Remember that the numbering of chapters and verses was not part of the original text of scripture. Jesus' description of the end times does not end with the final verse of Luke 17, but continues with parables of the kingdom in Luke 18. In those parables, it is clear that the day of the coming of the Son of Man is to be a day when justice is finally granted (vv. 1-8) and the self-righteous put in their place (vv. 9-14).

Like the widow in the first parable, we seek justice from unjust judges. Like the tax collector in the second parable, we are justified while those who exalt themselves are humbled. So the coming of the Son of Man is a good thing!

We pray for the day of justice and justification when every valley will be exalted, and every mountain made low, to prepare the way of our God. (Isaiah 40:3-4)

> *"The peasantry prospered in Israel,*
>   *they grew fat on plunder,*
> *because you arose, Deborah,*
>   *arose as a mother in Israel."*
> Judges 5:7

"Old" has to count for something, and the Song of Deborah (Judges 5) is believed the oldest text in the Bible, dating around 1125 B.C.E. The NRSV translates the Hebrew referring to Deborah in Judges 4:4 as "wife of Lappidoth," but the *HarperCollins Bible Dictionary* suggests it might also be translated "spirited woman." Since there's no sign of a "Lappidoth," the alternate translation fits better this woman who combined three roles: judge, military leader, and prophet. She was praised in all three roles. And she wasn't a bad lyricist either.

Though not directly part of Jesus' lineage, she certainly is part of his spiritual ancestry. The peasantry prospered in Israel when Jesus arose as well. "Blessed are you who are poor," Jesus said, "for yours is the kingdom of God" (Luke 6:20). Unlike Matthew's Sermon on the Mount, Jesus here doesn't say "poor in spirit." And in Luke, Jesus did not speak from a "mount" of authority, but "came down with them and stood on a level place, with a great crowd" (6:17). Jesus was so "PC" he could have led a politically inclusive National Gay & Lesbian Task Force event.

Not only did Jesus lift up the poor, who followed him in great numbers, but he questioned the privilege of the rich in sayings and parables: the rich man sent to Hades and the beggar Lazarus resting in the bosom of Abraham; the rich putting money into the Temple treasury compared to the poor woman who gave all she had; the rich man who piled high his wealth but whose soul would be required that night. When a ruler asked him how to inherit eternal life and was told to give his wealth to the poor, Jesus said, "it is easier for a camel to go through the eye of a needle than for someone who is rich to enter the kingdom of God" (Luke 18:25). This strong statement is then modified ("What is impossible for mortals is possible for God," Luke 18:27), but some scholars believe this loophole (as true as it is) was added by the early church to accommodate its rich patrons.

To translate this into our context, it is easier to come out as lesbian, gay, bisexual, or transgender and "enter the kingdom" before we accumulate things that we would fear losing if we do. And those things we gather around us—wealth, reputation, prestige, privilege, position, power, religiosity, and the rest—will insulate us from the work Jesus and his spiritual forebear Deborah call us to do.

Help me discern what I have that insulates me from others' needs and prevents me from serving them.

> *Letters were sent wishing peace and security to all the Jews.* Esther 9:30

These letters came from Queen Esther and her foster father, Mordecai, after a difficult chapter of Jewish history in Persia. A pogrom to kill her people had been in the works, and, risking her own death, Esther had decided to "come out" as a Jew to her husband the king to save her people. Thus was Purim established, a festival of victory and celebration and gift-giving in joyful memory of their salvation.

"Go therefore and make disciples of all nations. . . . And remember, I am with you always, to the end of the age," were the final words of Jesus to his disciples (Matthew 28:19–20). Just as the Word had come in flesh, so Jesus' words would come in the flesh of his disciples, retelling his stories, recounting his insights, writing them down, interpreting his life, and circulating their own "letters" to all the Christians, of their time and ours. These letters offer us a certain peace and security, even as we argue and divide over their further interpretation.

Because, as Esther stood in solidarity with her people, risking her own life, so Jesus stands in solidarity with us, having risked his life, yet maintaining his visibility and vision in us. Jesus risks being broken again as his Spirit leads us into further truth, but we have the promise that he will nonetheless be with us until the end of the age.

Jesus, thank you for being with us and with those who interpret the Bible differently than we. We pray for yet another resurrection of your Body, restoring us to one another, overcoming our divisions, your present wounds.

> *God has told you, O mortal, what is good;*
>   *and what does the LORD require of you*
> *but to do justice, and to love kindness,*
>   *and to walk humbly with your God?*
> Micah 6:8

Whatever else one believes, Jesus was a great prophet in the same spiritual line as all the Hebrew prophets. Together they proclaimed God's mercy and grace, God's awesomeness and God's righteousness. Thus they admonished us to do justice, especially for the outcast and deprived, and to be merciful and humble. This was true worship.

"The hour is coming when you will worship God neither on this mountain nor in Jerusalem. . . . The hour is coming, and is now here, when the true worshipers will worship God in spirit and truth," Jesus told the Samaritan woman at the well (John 4:21, 23). The trappings of religion—the Law, the sabbath, religious authorities, ritual, even the Temple itself—were being judged in a different light, by a different standard, that Jesus had brought into the world. His was a radical faith in a loving God, which sought our love for God and our neighbor.

What Christians made of this different light was another set of religious trappings—biblical literalism, legalism, fundamentalism, religious authorities, ritual, even the church itself. Yet "the true light, which enlightens everyone, was coming into the world," John wrote (John 1:9), and, though "the light shines in the darkness, . . . the darkness [can] not overcome it" (1:5).

John also wrote, "What has come into being in [the Word] was life, and the life was the light of all people" (1:3–4). We could reverse this saying: Jesus' *light* was also our *life*, releasing us from religious trappings that bind us and blind us rather than inspire us.

So we turn to contemplate that light in the season of Epiphany, which begins tomorrow.

You have told me, O God, what is good. What you require of me is to seek justice, to love kindness, and to walk humbly with you.

PART TWO

Unbearable Light

Meditations for Epiphany

Introduction

In general, epiphanies are unexpected revelations—"aha!"s. In religion and mythology, epiphanies are manifestations of divinity or the gods. In Christian faith, epiphany is a season commemorating revelations of Jesus' divinity. I use all three understandings in what follows.

The season of Epiphany begins with the visit of the Magi on January 6, when the divine nature of the Christ-child was revealed to priests of a foreign religion, and runs through the Transfiguration of Jesus on a mountain, witnessed by Peter and John and James, when "the appearance of his face changed, and his clothes became dazzling white" (Luke 9:29).

On the Sunday following January 6, Jesus' baptism is remembered, when a voice from heaven confirmed his divine nature. At one time, Jesus' birth, the visit of the Magi, Jesus' baptism, and his first miracle, at the wedding of Cana, were all observed on January 6. The end of Epiphany is determined each year by the beginning of Lent, on Ash Wednesday.

Enough meditations are provided here for the longest possible season of Epiphany. Lent is a movable feast. On the day before Ash Wednesday, skip to March 7, which reflects on the Transfiguration, then begin Part Three on Ash Wednesday.

The Sunday preceding Ash Wednesday is Transfiguration Sunday.

The season of Epiphany is the season of light, when God's divine light was breaking into the world. As a season of revelation, one could view it as a period celebrating God's *coming out* to us. As Moses could testify from his experience on Mount Sinai, God's coming out, God's divine light, is unbearable. Moses had wanted to see God, but God said no human could do so and live. So God held a hand over Moses' eyes while passing by, and Moses caught only a glimpse of God's "afterglow," as it were—God's backside. Moses' face glowed from his mountaintop experience so much that his fellow Israelites could not bear it, making him wear a veil over his face until the effect wore off.

There is another way in which the light of God is unbearable. It is impossible to "bear" it to others, that is, to adequately bear witness to the light. When the lightbulb goes on over your head with some clarifying insight, think how difficult it is to convey the power and significance of your "aha" experience to someone else. Even more so with God's unbearable light. Another can show you God's light only by reflection or indirection. An epiphany is very much in the eye, or experience, of the beholder. Thus descriptions about epiphanies, whether in scripture or in books of meditations like this, require readers to "suspend disbelief" to enter into the experience, just as theatergoers do when they enter into a dramatic performance.

There's more to light than first meets the eye. Light has its own epiphany. Light contains all the colors of the spectrum, revealed through light's refraction and dispersion through such things as raindrops and prisms. Light's diaspora is our rainbow. Our community has embraced the rainbow flag to suggest beauty and diversity, creativity and celebration. Thus we have welcomed the hidden meaning of light. We no longer long for some place "*over* the rainbow": we live *in* the rainbow. With Noah and his family, we look to the rainbow as a sign of God's covenant with us.

To see God's light requires eyes of faith. One does not have to be sighted to "see" God's light. But one does need to be visionary. Being visionary may be a gift, but it may also be a cultivated ability. Spiritual habits may sensitize us, developing our visionary ability. Just as one who works out regularly at a gym may be able to lift a weight he never thought possible, or one who studies a craft may accomplish a creation beyond her dreams, so spiritual disciplines may lead us to see epiphanies we thought were only for mystics.

Daily reflection on the epiphanies that surround us hones the sharpness of our senses. As we become accustomed to noticing the sacred, we begin to see it popping out all over the place, even in circumstances where we once would have seen only dark clouds with no silver linings, let alone rainbows of God's promise to be with us always.

> *When you read this you can perceive my insight
> into the mystery of Christ, which was not made
> known to the human race in other generations as
> it has now been revealed to Christ's holy apostles
> and prophets by the Spirit; that is, how the Gen-
> tiles are joint heirs, members of the same body,
> and partakers of the promise in Christ Jesus
> through the gospel.* Ephesians 3:4–6

Spiritual mysteries unfold. That's why new generations still
find ancient sacred texts meaningful, while interpreting
them so differently. That's why different cultures and peoples
and different *kinds* of people interpret them in diverse ways.
And that's why interpretations must be regarded as provi-
sional, tentative, partial, and thus proclaimed humbly.

The first Christians—Jews, for the most part, and, in this
instance, the apostle Paul—enjoyed a moment of epiphany
when, wrapped in the mystery of Christ, they realized
Christ's promise was for everyone, even those Gentiles
whom the Jews regarded as impure, sinful, heretical. Contemporary Christians have enjoyed a similar moment when
they have understood that Christ's promise is even for people
who are lesbian, gay, bisexual, and transgender.

It's not surprising that such epiphany would cause trouble in today's church, just as Paul's and Peter's (Acts 10)
epiphany stirred controversy in the early church. Yet such
inbreakings of God's Spirit are what unfolds the arms of the
mystical Body of Christ to welcome LGBT folk home to
God's promise of steadfast love. And, as we come home to
God, we add sinews, muscles, bone, brain, and heart to what

was always intended to be a living organism, not a mere organization.

May the church receive insight into the mystery of Christ, which was not made known to the human race in other generations as it has now been revealed to Christ's holy apostles and prophets by the Spirit: that is, how lesbians and gays, bisexuals, and transgenders are joint heirs, members of the same body, and partakers of the promise in Christ Jesus through the gospel.

JANUARY 7

Arise, shine; for your light has come,
*   and the glory of God has risen upon you....*
Then you shall see and be radiant;
*   your heart shall thrill and rejoice.* Isaiah 60:1, 5

There are those of us who prefer shadow to sunshine. We embrace what we believe to be the "dark side" of our personalities, accepting as inevitable sexual-spiritual alienation. But to God, to speak of our dark side is like speaking of the dark side of the moon. Just because we can't see the dark side of the moon doesn't mean it's not there and not absolutely necessary for the moon to exist. God sees and knows that all the parts of ourselves are necessary for survival.

But in the spiritual life, mere survival is not the goal. Remember Jesus' temptation to turn stones to bread in his hunger in the wilderness. What Isaiah describes is not mere survival, but glory, radiance, and rejoicing. Inadvertently wise, we sometimes refer to our sexual adventures as "cheap thrills." Lord knows, we've turned a lot of "stones" into "bread," a lot of less than fulfilling encounters and behaviors and relationships into manna to survive in the wilderness, losing our vision of the Promised Land. The hunger for cheap thrills may mask the hunger for a more costly thrill, intimacy. With those we love. With God.

"Cheap thrills" are not necessarily bad. They may even serve as signposts to a deeper reality and deeper needs. But to mistake them for the goal is spiritually shortsighted.

Even in the shadows, may I see the glory that I am and the glory of others. Lead me from the easy temptation to judge myself and others. Yet help me to discern what enhances the sacred glory you have given. "Open my eyes that I may see, glimpses of glory you have for me."

> *When they saw the star, they rejoiced exceedingly with great joy; and going into the house they saw the child with Mary his mother, and they fell down and worshiped him. Then, opening their treasures, they offered the child gifts, gold and frankincense and myrrh.* Matthew 2:10–11

Gay humor has it that this proves the Magi from the East were gay, because they stopped along their journey to the infant Jesus to go shopping!

Our culture, and particularly gay culture, pays attention to stars—celebrities who dot our culturescape, fundraisers, and movement. Andy Warhol's now famous truism that everyone may have his or her fifteen minutes of fame has made celebrities even of people who have done only one thing or had one thing done to them. Some of those "things" are truly of value, others may have little value but be "news-worthy," that is, sensational, catching media attention. Even victims have become famous.

Forgive and indulge me as I mention a pet peeve, one about our gay community and one about the culture at large. We give human rights awards to legislators who do their job by casting just one vote for our rights, while we ignore the people in the trenches of our gay rights organizations who made that vote happen. And morning programs and talk shows invite celebrities to pontificate on everything from personal relationships to spirituality, rather than invite the experts in those fields to comment.

The Magi are remembered because they followed the right star. Discernment is paramount in choosing to whom we pay attention and whom we adore—whether as spiritual guides, role models, political leaders, or movement strategists.

Forgive my "heresy," Jesus, but I believe it's not as spiritually vital how I understand your place in the cosmos as it is to allow you to touch my heart and lead my will to do what God wills. May you be my foremost guiding star in my spiritual quest.

And having been baptized, Jesus went up immediately from the water, and behold, the heavens were opened and Jesus saw the Spirit of God descending like a dove, and alighting on him; and lo, a voice from heaven, saying, "This is my beloved Child, with whom I am well pleased." Matthew 3:16–17

Imagine yourself as Jesus in this scene of his baptism at the hands of John. You set down your bag and strip yourself. You wade naked into the water. John holds you in his arms as he lowers you in the refreshing water and brings you up again, the water dripping from your hair, your skin, your nipples, your genitals, your buttocks. Through drops of the Jordan still in your eyes, you see the glimmering sun as if for the first time. Serendipitously a dove appears and lands on your head, as if it is welcome. And you hear a voice—a still, small, but sure voice—whisper on the wind, "This is my beloved Child, with whom I am well pleased."

This is why Jesus appeared on this earth. To remind us of our inheritance as creations of God, God's daughters and sons, inheritors of the commonwealth of God. To call us back to ourselves, to remind us of our first birth, and for us to be reborn in the waters of baptism. So we can discover the sacred that we are. Think of skinny-dipping as a youth or jumping naked into a private pool with a lover or friends—the playfulness and exuberance and innocence we are in that moment. That is the joy of spiritual rebirth—letting go of past heaviness, sorrow, sickness, and sin, at least for the moment. Enjoying "the unbearable lightness of being."

It's a shame that we are usually baptized only once, un-like Communion, which we receive again and again. Because we can be born again each and every day. The Holy Saturday/ Easter Vigil in some Christian traditions includes a sprinkling reminder of our baptisms. And every baptism we witness invites us to remember and reflect on our own, even if we were mere infants.

But to have our whole bodies, naked and vulnerable, immersed in God's watery womb again and again would remind us that we, our bodies, are sacred.

Naked, vulnerable, willing, letting go, repenting, I dive beneath your water's surface, Holy God, to feel your cleansing and refreshing caress, renewing my strength to live as your beloved Child, coming up out of the water, revived, to bask in the warmth of your proudly beaming smile.

> *From that time Jesus began to preach, saying,*
> *"Repent, for the realm of God is at hand." ...And*
> *Jesus went about all Galilee, teaching in their syn-*
> *agogues and preaching the gospel of the realm*
> *of heaven, and healing every disease and every*
> *infirmity among the people.* Matthew 4:17, 23

Of course, Jesus' preaching and healing did not follow his baptism immediately. He faced a wilderness of distractions and temptations and doubt. But Jesus' ability to speak of God's kingdom, realm, or commonwealth grew from this baptismal glimpse of the eternal—in the cosmos, in himself, in others.

That's why, if we're to keep sight of the eternal, we need daily baptism, if only a baptism of inspiring words and prayerful silence that reminds us what life is all about. Like Jesus, what we do for others grows out of our awareness of God's wish that no one be neglected, that everyone feel included. Repenting of indifference, ignorance, exploitation, prejudice, and hatred, we turn to touch the wounded of the world—the self-hating, the poor, the sick, the imprisoned, the addicted, the hungry, the homeless, the marginalized— through our volunteering, our votes, our offerings and dona-tions, our involvement, even our conversation.

Meditation and prayer is where it all begins. To remember our call and our destinies, we must spend time every day con-templating the uniqueness of our selves, our lives, and the selves and lives of others. Spiritual amnesia is the greatest threat to world peace and inner peace. Prayer is a time to re-member the world as God's, as God's kingdom, as God's realm, as God's commonwealth. Proclamation and healing then flow naturally.

Give us this day our daily "wake-up call" that we are important and vital in your mission, Jesus. May your eternal realm touch others through our hands and hearts, our help and healing. In lovemaking, make us gentle. In prayermaking, make us humble. In proclaiming the gospel, make us boldly inclusive.

> *Now standing there were six stone water jars for*
> *the Jewish rites of purification, each holding*
> *twenty or thirty gallons. Jesus said to them, "Fill the*
> *jars with water. . . . Now draw some out, and take*
> *it to the chief steward." . . . When the steward tasted*
> *the water that had become wine . . .* John 2:6–9

That's when the wedding at Cana really took off! Dionysus, god
of fertility and sensual ecstasy, eat your heart out! Just as water
allegedly turned to wine in Dionysian temples, Jesus transformed baptismal water set aside for the stodgy ritual of "baptizing" hands into celebration and revelry. And, gay gourmets,
please note his choice of wine was superb: "But you have kept
the good wine until now," the wine critic (steward) says.

By so doing, Jesus celebrated a sexual relationship. Yes, a
covenant relationship, but a covenant sexual relationship. So
sex is a good thing. "What Would Jesus Do?" doesn't answer
every question about what's holy. Jesus may have been celi-
bate, but he could enjoy and bless another person's sexuality by his presence at a wedding and his unique and sensual
wedding gift.

By tradition, this was Jesus' first miracle, transforming the
ordinary into the extraordinary, transforming the means of
mere survival (water) into the means of radiance and rejoicing (wine). And the fact that it was water intended for rites
of purification, thus dedicated to a holy purpose, suggests a
connection with our own baptismal waters. Our own baptism is intended not for mere survival (salvation, deliverance,
liberation) but for radiance and rejoicing and blessing
(proclamation and celebration of God's realm).

Transform our baptismal water into Communion wine, so we may glory in the taste of your Commonwealth, where you make your home with us, wiping away tears, welcoming every stranger, teaching us to dance, celebrating our sexuality, blessing our marriages.

JANUARY 12

And God said, "Let there be light"; and there was light. And God saw that the light was good. Genesis 1:3–4

This part of the creation story implies that light is virtually inherent in the cosmos. Epiphany is the season of light, a celebration of the revealed glory of God, the universe, Jesus, the earth, and its creatures, including us. The Big Bang theory of cosmic origin—which requires as much faith as does the notion that the cosmos was divinely inspired—suggests an explosion of light that came from a single point of origin, a single event.

So epiphanies, when that "lightbulb" goes on over our heads, have natural precedent. It is the way of things. When we realized our sexual or gendered difference or that of someone we loved, the light went on in our closets. Until that moment, our inklings of our "queer" realities may have seemed shadowy and scary. "Darkness was upon the face of the deep", as it was before God created light. Yet "the Spirit of God was moving over the face of the waters" and called for LIGHT. Light that was good. Self-realization. Our light. Our light not hidden by a bushel-basket closet, but set on a lampstand to bring yet more light into our world. A light that dispelled the scary, shadowy stuff for others. Epiphanies beget epiphanies.

Thank you, God, for your good light, which illumines the darkest places: our minds, our hearts, our closets, our churches. Your good light finds the cracks in our armored hiding places, slips around the corners and edges of our walls, sinks into the deepest crevices and caverns and pits in which we find ourselves. Let there be more *light, O God!*

> *Moses did not know that the skin of his face shone*
> *because he had been talking with God. When*
> *Aaron and all the Israelites saw Moses, the skin*
> *of his face was shining, and they were afraid to*
> *come near him.* Exodus 34:29–30

So Moses became the first cross-dresser in the Bible, wearing a veil over his face. Doubtless some of you will be wondering the fabric and dye and cut of the veil, but we're not given designer specifications.

Still, we know Moses' experience of having to wear the veil. We have learned how to edit and censor ourselves when it comes to proclaiming the glories of embracing our sexual and transgender natures. "Too much information," we call it. The apostle Paul would call it sparing the weaker brother or sister Christian our sense of freedom. He would also think it politic, because Paul himself became all things to all people in order to proclaim the gospel.

Yet our glorious freedom has also made me wonder if we really should struggle for full acceptance in the church or the general culture. Would such acceptance make us, or require us to be, as boring and inhibited as everyone else? I was sitting watching a comic drag show at the Armory in Atlanta when it came to me that Joe and Mary Presbyterian would never get nor accept this particular brand of humor—the edgy poking fun at ourselves, at cultural mores, at gender expectations, at the excesses and liabilities of our own sexuality. And I realized there is a lot that goes on in our community that might never be found "acceptable."

But audience regulars include a straight United Methodist

woman (whose husband happens to be a pastor) and a straight, elderly Jewish woman, both favorites of the performers. And soon after this experience, I met the straight Presbyterian sister of the man (alter ego, Thelma) who created the group performing, the Armorettes. She was deeply moved to visit Thelma's Pump Room and see her brother's ruby-red–sequined slippers in a place of honor. I guess with God all things are truly possible!

God, may the glow from our ruby-red–sequined slippers flash not only on stage but in the church, the workplace, and family gatherings. May we find more and more environments in which we can remove the veil of compliance with the strictures that straitjacket us all, being honest and inviting honesty so that together we may discern your glory in being human.

> *Moses did not know that the skin of his face shone because he had been talking with God. When Aaron and all the Israelites saw Moses, the skin of his face was shining, and they were afraid to come near him.* Exodus 34:29–30

No, the repetition of this text is not a mistake. Yesterday's scripture becomes today's because what's applicable to celebrating our sexuality is applicable to celebrating our spirituality.

We all know how difficult it is to remove the veil in the gay community so that the fact that we've been to church, or follow Jesus, or take time to pray does not inhibit our personal or political relations with other lesbian, gay, bisexual, or transgender people, many of whom have been spiritually abused by the church. We've seen too many a face darken at the mention of what we experience as the Light of the world.

When visitors come to Atlanta, I sometimes take them on Sunday nights to see the early part of the Armorettes show and the second show of the Gospel Girls. The latter is both uniquely Southern and unique to the South. Nowhere else have I seen gay men and lesbians join voices in rousing gospel tunes in a gay bar with the likes of Morticia DeVille (a large drag queen) and the Gospel Echos (a couple of gay men). Sometimes they lip-sync songs, but mostly they just sing. And there is an honest-to-goodness female African American whose vocals are extraordinary in range, beauty, and passion. Often, too, there are guest singers, who have performed that Sunday morning in worship services in the greater Atlanta area. Toward the end, there is a "high church singalong" of "Amazing Grace," led by volunteers in the audience.

Tears come to my eyes as I write about this, just as they often do when I witness it—because I know that for many of those present, this is their one chance on Sunday to sing the songs of faith on which they were reared, as well as their one opportunity to unabashedly sing of Jesus in the midst of gay people. Even those who may sing as if they're poking fun at religion know that the words and tunes still resonate in their souls.

Dear Jesus, may we find more and more opportunities to "sing God's song in a foreign land," bearing witness to your love and your light. As gay men so willingly strip off their shirts on the dance floor, may we, your people, strip off the veils that mask our souls that dance in you.

JANUARY 15

> *Since, then, we have such a hope, we act with great boldness, not like Moses, who put a veil over his face....Now the Lord is the Spirit, and where the Spirit of the Lord is, there is freedom. And all of us, with unveiled faces, seeing the glory of the Lord as though reflected in a mirror, are being transformed into the same image from one degree of glory to another; for this comes from the Lord, the Spirit.* 2 Corinthians 3:12–13, 17–18

Apologies for the noninclusive "Lord"! But "Sovereign" sounds severe; and "Christ" isn't accurate. And for nonwhites, and for the underprivileged of whatever color, "Lord" carries rich and kindly meanings. "Lord" here refers to Jesus, whom Christians early on identified with the Lord God. So, in this text, I decided not to adapt the language, remembering that well-meaning attempts to be gender-inclusive may exclude others.

The Spirit of Christ gives us the freedom to be bold in our hope. Thus, stripped of veils, we together as a community may witness the glory of God in one another's faces "as though reflected in a mirror."

Vividly I remember the first time I saw love in another boy's eyes. We were both in ninth grade, outside in the schoolyard, between classes. We were playfully hitting each other with our gloves when I caught the twinkle of love in his eyes as our gaze fixed on each other a brief eternity. There was nothing seductive about the glance; mere delight. How glorious it was to feel beloved! No matter that he later married and is presumably straight. He loved me for a moment, giving me what I had always wanted, and I was forever changed. To be beloved is transforming. To behold it in another's face is to witness the glory of Divine love "as though reflected in a mirror."

That's why we are called to be open about our love—so that others may see Jesus' and God's love reflected in our faces and recognize their own belovedness. And we must do this together so that we may grow into our glory as the beloved and as the community of the Beloved.

Thank you for the freedom of transformation in love—the ease with which we let go of past hurts and humiliations, habits, and hideouts when another's glorious love welcomes our glory. And to think such glory is a mere reflection of your glory, O God!

JANUARY 16

*And the word of God was rare in those days; there
was no frequent vision.* 1 Samuel 3:1

Thus begins the story of the calling of the prophet Samuel,
a mere boy who served the aging priest Eli, whose family was
corrupt and would be replaced. God called "Samuel! Samuel."
And, to give Eli his due, it was he who sagely told the boy that
it was God calling and instructed him to answer, "Speak, for
your servant hears." Thus Samuel learned of the downfall of
Eli's house and the rise of new spiritual leadership. Eli sounds
resigned to God's judgment when he pries it out of Samuel.

Gay boys and girls are being called by God at the very
moment you are reading this. Bisexual and transgender girls
and boys are too. Is the church likely to have the wisdom to
tell them they are hearing God's voice? The church is not as
resigned as Eli to God's judgment of its heterosexism and
transgenderphobia.

God is lifting up new spiritual leadership in the church
that will reform it. It is you who read this who must serve as
mentor to our youth, who need to know that God not only
has not abandoned them but is speaking to them and speaking through them, calling them to serve as prophets to the
church and culture—and to us.

*In the calling of our youth, may we hear our own calling
to serve as spiritual mentors and guides and models to the
succeeding generations of the church and of our movement. May they learn from us and may we learn from them
what it means to stand proudly gay in the world and yet
humbly human before you, our God.*

JANUARY 17

> *Now Mount Sinai was wrapped in smoke,*
> *because God had descended upon it in fire; the*
> *smoke went up like the smoke of a kiln, while the*
> *whole mountain shook violently.* Exodus 19:18

In another context, Deuteronomy describes God as "a devouring fire" (Deuteronomy 9:3). Not all epiphanies, or divine manifestations, are pretty. Some are downright scary, such as when the Hebrews received the Ten Commandments at Mount Sinai.

In workshops I sometimes invite participants to contemplate a specific event when they felt spiritually fulfilled and at peace. One might expect that participants would recall a morning in their lover's arms, a stroll along the shore, a time of prayer in an awe-inspiring place. But sometimes participants recall a scene that might not seem conducive to a sense of well-being: sitting beside a hospital bed as a friend with AIDS breathes his last, or having an accident in which your driver lost control of her car, or being arrested in a gay rights demonstration.

Perhaps the burning bush gave Moses a taste for more startling revelations of the Holy. Certainly the plagues visited on Egypt and the waters of the Red Sea crashing down on their oppressors gave the Hebrews a sense of God's awesome power. Moses drew the short straw and was given the task to go up the mountain and see what God wanted. Little did he know, as we have already learned, that the experience would set him all aglow.

Awesome God, you and the world you have created frighten us sometimes. Transform the fear into wonder at your power and amazement at our own ability to cope, to confront, to challenge, and even to find meaning in those things we cannot control nor fully understand.

> *Then God said to Moses, "Go down and warn the
> people not to break through to God to look; oth-
> erwise many of them will perish." ... Moses said
> to God, "The people are not permitted to come up
> to Mount Sinai; for you yourself warned us, say-
> ing, 'Set limits around the mountain and keep it
> holy.'"* Exodus 19:21, 23

Like any celebrity, God wants some privacy, Mount Sinai spe-
cial effects notwithstanding. As revealing as God is, there are
limits to what we can know or experience of the Sacred.
Think of it—God even covered Moses' face passing by (Exodus 33:22)! That's why, when most of us think of epiphanies,
we think of mere glimpses of the sacred in our midst.

"I WILL BE WHAT I WILL BE," God mysteriously replies to
Moses' request for a name (Ex. 3:14, NRSV margin). That's
why, later, when Hebrew scriptures were read aloud, the
Hebrew word Adonai (Lord) was substituted for God's name
in the text. In those times, it was believed that to have or use
a god's name was to exercise power over the god. And, in any
time, to believe one has the power to know God fully leads
one into heresy, idolatry, fundamentalism, literalism, and
legalism.

We can't even know ourselves fully, let alone another person. We are attracted to our own mystery and the mystery of
others. It is through engagement that we learn more and
more about one another. This is true with God. Think of all
the pages in the Bible devoted to comprehending the divine
nature and God's relationship to us!

And don't we love a good mystery?

Good Mystery, you intrigue us, titillating us with traces of your presence in history and in nature, within community and within ourselves. As often as we sometimes cry, "Show yourself!" we also know we would die if your fullness were revealed to us. Thanks for holding back, preventing us from trampling on your holy space in our ignorance and in our pride.

> *Let me alone, for my days are a breath.*
> *What are human beings, that you make so much*
>   *of them,*
>   *that you set your mind on them,*
> *visit them every morning,*
>   *test them every moment?*
> Job 7:16–18

One of the most fantastic visions of God in the Bible comes to Job in the midst of questioning human suffering. Many of us can testify to our own experiences of divine presence and revelation in the midst of suffering.

In the closet, coming out, disowned by loved ones, losing friends and lovers to AIDS and breast cancer, missing out on jobs or promotions for who we are, being excommunicated by our spiritual communities, enduring the stress and debilitation and pain of life-threatening illness—many of us have suffered great pain. Some of us have followed Job's lead in questioning God. Others have been drawn closer to God when everyone else abandoned us.

God's response to Job is hardly satisfying to those who suffer:

Where were YOU when I laid the foundation of the earth?
   Tell me, if you have understanding.
Who determined its measurements—surely YOU know! . . .
   or who laid its cornerstone
when the morning stars sang together
   and all the heavenly beings shouted for joy?"

                     (Job 38:4–7, emphasis mine)

In other words—put things in perspective, stop whining,* get on with life.

Yet there is a kind of beauty and wonder in God's answer—the beauty and wonder of the cosmos, even when we don't understand the whys and wherefores of our little lives. And more wonder and beauty as apparently our lives are not so little, because God makes so much of us, visiting us every morning, prodding and nudging us to be all that we can be, even in suffering.

Who am I, that you make so much of me, setting your mind on me, visiting me every morning, testing me every moment? Yet, as the Psalmist says, you have made me a little less than yourself, and crowned me with glory and honor. "O God, our Sovereign, how majestic is your name in all the earth!" (Psalm 8:4–5, 9)

* This may sound harsh if applied to the truly devestated. Here I am assuming my readers are not Holocaust survivors, former slaves, victims of apartheid, and so forth. Depicting our suffering as akin to that of the Holocaust, slavery, or apartheid overdramatizes our plight and does a disservice to those who suffered them.

> *There is no longer Jew or Greek, there is no longer*
> *slave or free, there is no longer male and female;*
> *for all of you are one in Christ Jesus.* Galatians 3:28

That there is "no longer male and female" is quite a realization coming out of a tradition that declared in Genesis 1:27 that "male and female God created them."

A few months ago, my dog Calvin and I found a stray puppy in the park we visit daily. We were unsuccessful at attempts to locate her owner, and Mrs. Hobbes has become a part of our previously all-male family. I am still having difficulties using the right pronouns, since I've gotten used to referring to Calvin as "he." Now I use the wrong pronouns for both of them, sometimes calling Calvin "she." The confusion is one more "aha" about how definitions of gender are socially defined. I remember as a child believing that dogs were the males and cats were the females! (I've learned others suffered from this same confusion.)

My dogs' favorite dogsitter is Erin Swenson. Erin has become a close friend, our friendship deepening as she helped me survive recent losses. Erin generously and graciously stays here in our home when I go out of town.

A few years ago, Erin was given her annual approval for her counseling ministry by the Presbytery of Greater Atlanta. This had not been a problem until she made the transition from Eric to Erin, and requested that her name be changed on the rolls of presbytery. (In the Presbyterian Church, ministers are members of their presbyteries, not their congregations.) Though we didn't really know each other then, I wanted to show my support by attending the presbytery meeting that would decide her fate. To my amazement, the vote, though close, was clearly in Erin's favor (and in God's favor too, I believe). Every once in a while the church surprises us by letting the Spirit in.

I had never known Erin as Eric, and I once confessed, "I can't even imagine you as a man!" "That's because I wasn't," she responded. She had always thought who she was inside differed from who she was outside.

As more and more transgender people "come out," "there is no longer male and female" takes on a whole new meaning. Indeed, many consider themselves transgender above considering themselves male or female. To think that the apostle Paul was so ahead of himself!

Thank you for the spectrum of gender between male and female! Just as you made light out of a spectrum of colors, so you have made our identities out of a spectrum of genders. May we see both spectrums as rainbows of promise and fulfillment. Amen.

JANUARY 21

> *"What God has made clean, you must not call profane."* Acts 10:15

This epiphany came in a dream Peter had about food that was considered impure by Jewish dietary laws. But it led to a greater epiphany: that no human being could be considered unclean, not even the Gentiles, who ate these unclean foods.

The Pharisees once criticized Jesus' disciples for not ritually baptizing their hands before eating. Jesus defended them, essentially saying: not what goes into a person, but what comes out of a person's heart is what is spiritually vital (see Matthew 15:1–20). Given Jesus' ministry to the outcasts of his time, we may easily justify the further refinement: not who a person is but what comes out of the person's heart.... Not form, but content, matters to God. No matter our sexual orientation, nor the gender of our partners. No matter our genitals, but the gender(s) we are deep within. What comes out of ourselves and our relationships is what counts.

God has made us, and made us clean. We are not "profane"—literally, "before the temple," that is, outside the temple, secular. Each of us is part of the temple: "Come to God, a living stone, though rejected by mortals yet chosen and precious in God's sight, and like living stones, let yourselves be built into a spiritual house" (1 Peter 2:4–5).

The religion into which Jesus was born was big on purity versus impurity. The religion into which we were born is big on purity versus impurity. To follow Jesus' and the Spirit's lead, we recognize that what is spiritually vital to us is not this us-versus-them, exclusive duality. What is spiritually vital, and much more demanding, is living out our God-given holiness.

That I am holy humbles me. I feel unworthy to have you in my home, but you are already there, healing my beloved, welcoming my return. Lead me home to my sacred self, created in your image, restored by your Child, nurtured by your Spirit.

JANUARY 22

The circumcised believers who had come with Peter were astounded that the gift of the Holy Spirit had been poured out even on the Gentiles, for they heard them speaking in tongues and extolling God. Acts 10:45–46

See what happens? You claim nothing is unclean that God has made, and there goes the neighborhood! The Gentiles will be moving right next door, sitting next to us in our pews, and—who knows?—probably demanding to proclaim the gospel from our pulpits. It's Pandora's box all over again! Who's next?

First it was "gays," then "lesbians," now it's "bisexuals" and "transgenders." Close the church door, quick, before anybody else gets in! The snowball has become an avalanche of people breaking down the doors to be a part of us!

What's wrong with this picture? The church that grew by stretching itself to be as inclusive as possible is curling itself into a defensive ball, like a frightened animal. Not risking to stretch its arms wide for fear of ending up like Jesus on his cross, the church misses the broader commonwealth of God to save its puny institutional life—the gospel be damned!

And I'm not writing here of our opponents, who are convinced that we are wrong. I'm writing of the moderate majority who are not convinced one way or another, but are willing to sacrifice us for the sake of denominational purity, unity, and peace.

But with Peter we ask, how "can anyone withhold the water for baptizing these people who have received the Holy Spirit just as we have?" (Acts 10:47).

And given our dwindling congregations, don't we need everybody who can confess Jesus as central to their faith?

Give us, your church, the boldness of Jesus welcoming the "unclean," the temerity of Peter baptizing the Gentiles, the audacity of Martin Luther standing on grace alone—no matter those who crucify, criticize, and excommunicate your prophets!

JANUARY 23

> *I appeal to you therefore, brothers and sisters, by the mercies of God, to present your bodies as a living sacrifice, holy and acceptable to God, which is your spiritual worship. Do not be conformed to this world, but be transformed by the renewing of your minds, so that you may discern what is the will of God—what is good and acceptable and perfect.* Romans 12:1-2

"Do not be conformed to this world" actually means "do not be conformed to this age." Just as we no longer practice slave trade, just as women are now to be treated as equal to men, so our faith is not confined to another age's conceptions of sexuality. What Paul thought of homosexuality is irrelevant; it's what God thinks.

Our minds and the minds of our friends as well as some former opponents have been changed about homosexuality and same-gender relationships. Together, we have discerned that our sexuality and our covenants are "good and acceptable and perfect" to God.

The more important part of this passage to me, however, is the locus of the sacred in our bodies. Sacrifices were "devoted" to God, thus sacred. So many Christians act as if their bodies are dirty, evil, and shameful. So many people treat their bodies in shameful ways, not proving good stewards of our most precious gift—the only gift that allows us to enjoy all God's other gifts: creation, other creatures, God. We pollute and exploit our own bodies in ways we would never pollute or exploit another's body.

Our true worship (a term made from root words meaning "create worth") is to regard and offer our bodies as sacred—

in lovemaking, in prayermaking, in doing good, in justice-seeking, and in peacemaking. Our bodies are holy. As such they reveal and reflect divine glory. Look at your body. Your hands. Your feet. Your arms. Your legs. Your neck. Your head. Your eyes. Your shoulders. Your chest. Your abdomen. Your groin. Your genitals. Your back. Your buttocks. Look at any missing or disabled parts, because those are part of your holiness too. Say to yourself as much as to God: "These are very good."

I am holy. My body reveals your glory, God. My breath is your breath. My body was shaped by your hands. In Christ, your blood flows through my veins. My mind reflects your wisdom. My senses taste your pleasure and feel your pain. My time line whispers the glory of your timelessness. My finite self is an undeniable point of your infinite self. What my body is and does has significance well beyond my imagination. Help me to discern "what is good and acceptable and perfect" to you.

> *I have told the glad news of deliverance*
> *in the great congregation;*
> *…I have not restrained my lips,*
> *as you know, O God.*
> *I have not hidden your saving help within my*
> *heart.*
> Psalm 40:9–10

The truth is, many of us who are lesbian, gay, and bisexual are more willing to talk about our sexuality and our sexual experiences than about our spirituality and spiritual experiences in *our* "great congregation," the gay community. Even in our church congregations, we may be hesitant to speak of our spiritual experiences. I have wondered if the observation about the era of the prophet Samuel's boyhood calling, that "The word of God was rare in those days; visions were not widespread" (1 Samuel 3:1), was more about people's reticence to share their visions than about any diminishing revelation.

Most of you reading this will know how easily dismissed we are when we bring our faith out of the closet, whether in a gay bar or in a gay political organization. Only recently has a major gay political group realized the power of organizing a religious roundtable to assist them in what is essentially a spiritual struggle for our rights.

Claiming one's faith these days is too often viewed as "soft" or "sentimental," even "hypocritical." Yet I know I could not have claimed my sexuality or justice so easily without my faith tradition. Seeking reform rather than revolution in the church and the culture is too often viewed as "tinkering" with unredeemable systems. Yet both humility and pragmatism persuade many of us that, at best, we can only *reform* the church and most institutions. Thus we do what we can.

In the "mean"time, we celebrate the "glad news" of what our faith has done for us and can do for others in giving us deliverance and saving help.

Thank you, Jesus, for your saving help, leading us on The Way to promised lands and spiritual commonwealths through inspiring visions and words. Make us evangelists, proclaiming your Good News in the LGBT community as well as the church, unashamed of your Gospel!

> *And immediately there was in their synagogue someone with an unclean spirit who cried out, "What have you to do with us, Jesus of Nazareth? Have you come to destroy us? I know who you are, the Holy One of God."* Mark 1:23–24

Once I heard someone introduced with the observation, "He has all the right enemies!" This is a version of Franklin Delano Roosevelt's counsel, "Judge me by the enemies I have." It should cheer us that we are opposed by the likes of Fred Phelps, Phyllis Schlafly, Pat Robertson, "Dr." Laura, Jerry Falwell, and Cardinal Ratzinger. Would we really *want* such people on our side? Would any of us recognize them as valid spiritual guides? Even unaccepting houses of worship distance themselves from such vitriolic responses to us.

Epiphanies sometimes come out of the mouths of demonic spirits, according to today's text and other Gospel stories in which Jesus' sacred self is acknowledged by unclean spirits while his disciples still didn't get it. If one believes that demons are angels gone bad, then maybe demons' fear of destruction comes from Jesus' very different choice. Think of our opponents in the so-called "ex-gay" movement, or our opponents who are either outed by their own behavior or finally come out—maybe their fear of us is that we are what they want to be, and they fear destruction of their present lives.

And, more broadly, we who affirm our sexual-spiritual integrity are frightening to churches that have inadequately integrated sexuality and spirituality, and even more fearsome to Christians who view sexuality and spirituality as opposing forces. To be the "holy one of God" is to be both "whole" and "sacred," and many who oppose us find our health and goodness disconcerting and dangerous. That most of our opposition don't even want us in their pews should serve as a sure sign to those in the middle that our opposition cannot be trusted in their views.

Jesus, in your name and with your authority, may we rebuke the spirits of homophobia and heterosexism, biphobia and transphobia, racism and sexism, ableism and ageism, that cause fear of your "new teaching" (Mark 1:27). *As you command these demonic forces to "Be silent, and come out!"* (1:25), *may the resulting convulsions* (1:26) *not destroy your church.*

JANUARY 26

> *"This day is holy to the LORD your God; do not mourn or weep." For all the people wept when they heard the words of the law. Then [Nehemiah and Ezra] said to them, "Go your way, eat the fat and drink sweet wine and send portions of them to those for whom nothing is prepared, for this day is holy to our LORD; and do not be grieved, for the joy of the LORD is your strength." So the Levites stilled all the people, saying, "Be quiet, for this day is holy; do not be grieved." And all the people went their way to eat and drink and to send portions and to make great rejoicing, because they had understood the words that were declared to them.*
> Nehemiah 8:9–12

Really hearing the word of God is a moving experience. Think of times when you have been deeply moved by the love of a friend, the death of a parent, the innocence of a child, the playfulness of a pet, the insight of a writer, the story of a preacher, a reading from scripture, a view from a mountain, the flight of a butterfly. I believe that the word of God comes in many forms, if only we have eyes to see, ears to hear, and hands to feel.

The people of Israel were deeply moved to hear the word of God addressed to them. Today widely diverse communities of faith hear the word of God in scripture personally addressed to them, and they too are moved.

A therapist friend once told me that tears are always a sign of grief. Even so-called "tears of joy" may represent some kind of grief: that joy is fleeting, that sorrow preceded the joy, that things should always be this way, that not everyone can share the joy. I believe it was tears not only of repentance but of joy that the people of Israel wept that day. That God would speak to *them*! And yet, in Yahweh's holy presence, how inadequate they felt, how many changes they wanted to make in their own lives and the life of their community.

But their spiritual leaders told them not to grieve about the past, but to take joy in God's strength, to eat and drink in celebration and send food and wine to others. May we also rejoice that we have heard God's words addressed personally to us, looking forward to the future rather than forlornly to the past. May we celebrate with food and drink and share our celebration with others.

Thanks for speaking to us, holy God. Sometimes we don't notice that you're talking or don't catch exactly what you have to say. Help us to be attentive. Help us not to fret or grieve over things we've missed, realizing such mourning only keeps us from hearing what you're saying to us now.

> *Once more Jesus spoke to them in parables, say-*
> *ing: "The kingdom of heaven may be compared to*
> *a king who gave a wedding banquet for his son....*
> *Then he said to his slaves, 'The wedding is ready,*
> *but those invited were not worthy. Go therefore*
> *into the main streets, and invite everyone you*
> *find to the wedding banquet.' Those slaves went*
> *out into the streets and gathered all whom they*
> *found, both good and bad; so the wedding hall*
> *was filled with guests."* Matthew 22:1–2, 8–10

Within the ellipsis of this text occurs much of the story. The king sends his servants to invite his guests to the wedding banquet. The guests not only refuse to come, they mistreat and kill the servants. So the king kills them and burns their city. Then he sends other servants to invite strangers. What follows verse 10 is the expulsion of one of these persons for wearing the wrong clothes!

The parable makes me squeamish, because the "king" in the parable doesn't match my conception of God, except in the welcome of strangers to the feast. Obviously, this parable must be read with a discerning soul. The whole point of the story is that God sent prophets to God's own to invite them to a holy celebration. When the prophets were martyred, God decided to open the invitation a little wider, with the exception of one who was tossed because he didn't show the proper reverence for the occasion (I guess).

Squeamishness aside, during the time I've been writing these meditations for Epiphany, I have been reading through Matthew during my morning prayers. And in the context of my life, I found a new meaning in this familiar story.

In one short year I coped with my mother's death and the death of three close friends, as well as my lover's decision to separate. Then followed a series of lesser but also aggravating events that rarely happen in anybody's life, let alone mine. I've felt very much alone. I've noticed a certain creeping curmudgeonry growing in me like the unwanted fungus that just killed my lawn. I recently read Gore Vidal's autobiography, *Palimpsest*, and admit to delighting in his skepticism and cynicism as a kind of quintessential curmudgeon, probably as a balance to my own Pollyanna tendencies. "Sweetness and light" people began to annoy me more than before.

It was in this context that I read this parable about the wedding banquet. In this (and I realized other parables) I heard God saying to me, "Come in to the party," and that has become my mantra whenever I sensed resentment, envy, bitterness, anger, or withdrawal bubbling up within me. I remembered the elder brother whose father begs him to come in to the party celebrating his prodigal brother's return, and the master who asserts his right to pay his servants equally though they were hired at different times of the day. Believe it or not, this simple little phrase has done much to get me over myself and into showing the proper reverence for the joy that is life.

All you ask is that we "come in to the party," showing the proper respect for your invitation and the occasion that is life. God, you do give a great party! May we invite yet others to your celebration. L'chayim! To life!

> *For just as the body is one and has many mem-*
> *bers, and all the members of the body, though*
> *many, are one body, so it is with Christ. For in the*
> *one Spirit we were all baptized into the one*
> *body—Jews or Greeks, slaves or free—and we*
> *were all made to drink of one Spirit.* 1 Corinthians
> 12:12–13

In my view, the central and vital epiphany of every spiritual path worth our passage is unity. To me, spirituality is about recognizing and valuing our connection with every creature and all creation. In the ultimate epiphany—the glaring light of divinity—boundaries disappear, gravity no longer holds, time is endless. This is the mystical experience, union. With God. With one another. With the cosmos.

The early Christians recognized and valued that they were one in Christ. That meant that differences that otherwise would have divided them no longer should. In Jesus' judgment parable in Matthew 25, early Christians saw their unity with the stranger in need, who is Christ "in a distressing disguise," to borrow a phrase from Mother Teresa. Paul would envision the creation unified by its "groaning in labor pains" awaiting fulfillment (Romans 8:22). And John's apocalypse in Revelation unveiled the Christian struggle as one for the unified soul of the world.

"Now we know in part," to paraphrase Paul in the chapter of 1 Corinthians that follows our passage above (13:12). Though Christians throughout the ages have glimpsed our connections to all, we have often seen such connection only in evangelical terms—with an eye to conversion "that they may be one, as we are one" as Christ prayed for his disciples in John 17:11. There is nothing wrong with wanting to share what's been good to us and for us. But it represents only a partial understanding of a greater truth.

Pluralism has always been the way of the world. Yet Christians are only beginning to accept that other faiths may have equal validity. Thus, while unity for confessing Christians is based in Christ, we must understand our unity with the cosmos in broader terms. We are made of the same divine starstuff. We are not all of Christ, but we are all of divine origin, whether you have faith in a Big Bang or a Grand God—or both.

Diverse in faith, in culture, in origin and condition, we all belong in God.

> *For as in one body we have many members, and*
> *not all the members have the same function, so*
> *we, who are many, are one body in Christ, and*
> *individually we are members one of another. We*
> *have gifts that differ according to the grace given*
> *to us.* Romans 12:4–6

I enjoy leading workshops and retreats because I love the interaction of the participants. I pleasured in a reported compliment at one such retreat, "He really is interested in what others have to say!" Though I would like to pride myself on my openness (and wish I could *always* be that way!), the fact of the matter is, since I spend the bulk of my time working alone, I am *desperate* to hear other people's voices and stories. What may be experienced as virtue is, in reality, necessary for my survival.

But I also have a philosophy behind my desire to make gatherings interactive. I believe the *collective* expertise is far more complete than my *individual* expertise. Even my so-called "individual" expertise is based on my years of hearing, reading, and reflecting with other people! I try to reflect back some of what I have learned, but I also anticipate that participants will do the same.

That, to me, is the essence of spiritual leadership. I first learned it during college from a progressive Baptist preacher. In a sermon he explained that he viewed his role as being paid to spend a little more time than the rest of his congregation listening to its members and reflecting back some of their individual spiritual growth, thus enabling the whole congregation to grow.

Everyone is a theologian. Everyone is an ethicist. Everyone is a mystic. Everyone does good, whether by charitable acts or by working for justice. And so on. Some of us may be better at one thing than another, but we are all involved in the spiritual and specifically Christian enterprise. That's why we need to listen up!

The reason much mainstream theology has been questioned in the last century is because it has been viewed as the enterprise of the few rather than the many. Thank God that new voices from different races, cultures, genders, sexualities, abilities, ages, and so forth have boldly spoken up. The more who express their perspective, the better we know God, one another, and ourselves.

Thank God it's not all up to me, nor the person with whom I disagree! You are beyond our knowledge, holy God. But our individual guesses collectively represent your mysteries and our histories. May I boldly add my voice where no one has gone before!

> *But speaking the truth in love, we must grow up in every way into him who is the head, into Christ, from whom the whole body, joined and knit together by every ligament with which it is equipped, as each part is working properly, promotes the body's growth in building itself up in love.* Ephesians 4:15–16

Christian unity is not mindless. We have an organizing principle, a director, a guide. We look to Jesus because we believe he somehow got it right. Love God and love neighbor were his basic tenets, though applications may vary. Yet we also listen for the Spirit to lead us beyond what the historical Jesus knew and spoke about. Jesus comforted his disciples by speaking of this Spirit that would lead them into "all the truth" because they could not "bear" the many things that Jesus had to say (John 16:12–13).

Neither do I believe that cosmic unity is mindless. Only God knows its organizing principle, but it could be said to be *relationship*, from molecule to universe; or *energy*, from "simple" gravity to life; or *experimentation*, endless variations that have resulted in everything from black holes to the rainbow spectrum of life on our own planet—or all of the above or none of the above! Obviously I am not a scientist, but I'm intrigued by scientific inquiry that quests for such answers.

The spiritual inquiry is a quest for answers too. Too many people settle for dogma and doctrines and canon rather than struggle for all the truth. Today in my morning prayers I was reading Matthew's account of Jews demanding the crucifixion of Jesus and the release of Barabbas (Matthew 27:11–26). I found the account almost wholly unbelievable, except metaphorically, the way we often crucify our own, no matter what community we belong to. I doubted that the Jews would actually ask their oppressors to execute one of their own. If the Jews wanted to apply the death penalty for blasphemy, Jesus would have been stoned. Of course I'm aware that the Gospel writers were biased toward Rome, because that was the direction of their evangelism.

When I was a "weaker" Christian (see entry for March 2), even thinking such a thought would have terrified me. What I've come to know, however, is that my salvation is not dependent on orthodoxy. It's dependent on seeking all the truth. In my Christian faith, Jesus and the Holy Spirit are my guides. And even in error, God's grace is my salvation.

Free us from closets that box in our thinking and our loving and our living. Open us to your Spirit, who blows where she will, leading us into more truth than we could stand before. You yourself, God, are not confined by churches or canon, dogma or doctrine. You're flying somewhere out there where we cannot capture you. You're springing up somewhere inside us where we cannot contain you.

> *But God has so arranged the body, giving the*
> *greater honor to the inferior member, that there*
> *may be no dissension within the body, but the*
> *members may have the same care for one*
> *another. If one member suffers, all suffer together*
> *with it; if one member is honored, all rejoice*
> *together with it.* 1 Corinthians 12:24–26

How delicate Paul becomes, we might think. Perhaps not. What *is* the "inferior member"? When I read this as a fundamentalist youth, I assumed it was the genitals. There was a reason for this, because Paul earlier writes, "Those members . . . we think less honorable we clothe with greater honor." Yet there is ambiguity here, lest we think of *any* member of our human bodies as necessarily inferior.

Sexually, we may have our own hierarchy of body parts, relative to the gender or genders to which we are attracted. That may prevent us from fully appreciating other parts of the body and paying attention to them in lovemaking.

Spiritually we have often been taught a hierarchy of body parts that may prevent us from fully appreciating parts of our bodies in our prayermaking. For some Christians, the head has ascendancy as the place of reason. For others, the heart comes first as the locus of feelings. The groin area doesn't even come into play, so to speak, unless it is to be controlled by the head (letting it be controlled by the heart is considered too risky!).

The church itself has a hierarchy of parts within the Body of Christ which prevents it from fully appreciating all its parts. Thus it suffers many self-inflicted disabilities because it resists using a muscle here or a tendon there, a toe here or a finger there. Hebrew scriptures use "stiff-necked" to indicate "stubborn." Applied to the Body of Christ, a stubborn church may be cutting off most of the Body of Christ from the head, much as a neck injury may cause paralysis because of insufficient "communication" between the brain and the body.

Dear Jesus, your Body suffers because we suffer in a hierarchy of who's important and who's expendable. Re-call the church to honor all its members so we may all rejoice together.

FEBRUARY 1

> *So faith, hope, love abide, these three; but the greatest of these is love.* 1 Corinthians 13:13

You can have any or all of the gifts of the Holy Spirit. You can have faith to move mountains. You can perform every act of charity and justice-making under the sun. But if you do not love, you are nothing and gain nothing.

In this famous "love" chapter written by the apostle Paul, he does not contrast love to materialism, idolatry, greed, lust, violence, or any grievous act or way of life. Paul contrasts love with good and godly things: spiritual gifts, unquestioned faith, sacrificing altruism. All those good and godly things, he writes, come to nothing if not in the service of love.

Then Paul describes love in terms associated with non-possessiveness, summed up in "Love does not insist on its own way" (1 Corinthians 13:5).

Most of us have doubted God at one time or another because we say, "Why isn't God more evident in the world? Why doesn't God answer all our doubts in a straightforward way?" Well, think about it. If God lived next door, what freedom would you have? Wouldn't you feel compelled to develop your spiritual gifts, to question nothing in your faith, and to give sacrificially to others? After all, who can say no to God?

God does not insist on God's own way. That's why God's love leaves us alone, bearing all things we do, believing all things we doubt, hoping all things for our good, enduring all the ways we resist love. Because God does not want to coerce us. God rather rejoices in our choices to love.

Now we know in part; then shall we understand fully, even as we have been fully understood.

Help me to be patient and kind, not jealous or boastful, nor arrogant or rude. Help me not to insist on my own way; not to be irritable or resentful; not to rejoice at wrong, but rejoice in the right. Help me to bear all things, believe all things, hope all things, endure all things.

> *"Holy, holy, holy is the God of hosts;*
> *the whole earth is full of God's glory."*
> *And the foundations of the thresholds shook at*
> *the voice of the one who called, and the house was*
> *filled with smoke.* Isaiah 6:3–4

After hearing the six-winged seraphim sing this gloria, feeling the foundations of the Temple shake, and seeing it fill with smoke around God, sitting high and mighty on a throne and wearing a royal robe with a train that filled the place, no wonder Isaiah exclaimed, "Woe is me! For I am lost; for I am a person of unclean lips, and I dwell in the midst of a people of unclean lips; for my eyes have seen the King, the God of hosts!" (Isaiah 6:5).

Rarely do epiphanies come in such Hollywood spectacle, offscreen chorus accompanied by THX ("The Audience Is Listening") Surroundsound that shakes the floor beneath our feet, Spielberg clouds unrolling before our eyes, and God sporting a train that would make Priscilla, Queen of the Desert, envious!

And that lip thing! I don't know about you, but I'd need a ton of burning coals to clean mine! And I'm not talking about the things I did for love. I'm talking about the hurtful or ignorant or unjust things I've said. I'm talking about my "less than righteous" anger, or my need to direct, or my greedy lust.

But after one of the seraphim anointed his lips with a burning coal, Isaiah was able to attend to God's plea, "Whom shall I send, and who will go for us?" and respond, "Here am I! Send me."

Though our epiphanies will probably never be like this, we too are invited by whatever glimpses of God's glory we encounter, to be sent, to "go" for God to our people, to God's people, and share our epiphanies.

Here I am! Send me! Whatever insights into the glory that is life that you've given me, I will proclaim. Bless my mouth with the right thing to say at the right time to the person who most needs to hear it.

> *And when the ass saw the angel of the LORD, she
> fell down under Balaam: and Balaam's anger was
> kindled, and he smote the ass with a staff. And the
> LORD opened the mouth of the ass, and she said
> unto Balaam, What have I done unto thee, that
> thou hast smitten me these three times? And Ba-
> laam said unto the ass, Because thou hast mocked
> me: I would there were a sword in mine hand, for
> now would I kill thee....Then the LORD opened the
> eyes of Balaam, and he saw the angel of the LORD
> standing in the way, and his sword drawn in his
> hand: and he bowed down his head, and fell flat
> on his face.* Numbers 22:27–29, 31 (KJV)

O.K., you *know* why I selected the King James Version of this story. Just so I could say, even an ass may see an epiphany we don't!

Balaam was called on by enemies of the people of Israel to curse God's people. Though himself a diviner, he could not see an angel who stood in his way. His donkey came to his rescue.

Like it or not, we have to admit that occasionally an ass has come to our rescue or prevented us from doing something we would regret. Maybe a boor, a geek, someone obnoxious, an arrogant person, an opponent, a "devil's advocate," an "ignoramus," a know-it-all, someone too cheery, a participant of an "intervention," a curmudgeon, a naysayer, a Pollyanna—whatever our definition of an "ass," often dependent on our own mood at the time. Occasionally even the most annoying person has something to say to us that we need to hear, or gives us an insight or solution for a challenging situation, or offers us an opportunity for spiritual growth.

And sometimes, truth be told, we play that role for others!

If Balaam's ass can see an angel, epiphanies are not limited to everyday people, let alone mystics and "diviners"! And those who think of themselves as having spiritual or psychic gifts like Balaam might realize that they too have blind spots.

Sacred Stranger, open my mind and heart to the epiphanies of others, even those whom I might not like at the time, or at all!

FEBRUARY 4

> *Now as he was going along and approaching Damascus, suddenly a light from heaven flashed around him. He fell to the ground and heard a voice saying to him, "Saul, Saul, why do you persecute me?" He asked, "Who are you, Lord?" The reply came, "I am Jesus, whom you are persecuting. But get up and enter the city, and you will be told what you are to do." Acts 9:3–6*

Now as Fred Phelps was going along and approaching another occasion where he planned an antigay demonstration, suddenly a light from heaven flashed around him. He fell to the ground and heard a voice saying to him, "Fred, Fred, why do you persecute me?" He asked, "Who are you, Lord?" The reply came, "I am Jesus, whom you are persecuting. But get up and go to San Francisco, and you will be told what to do."—From my own "Much Later Acts of the Apostles."

Notice how this follows on the heels of the discussion of Balaam's ass yesterday. You may insert any of our opponents' names into this imagined scenario. You may even wish to insert your own pastor's name, or a family member's name, or the name of a friend or coworker.

Now insert your own name.

Do this because most of us also had that conversion experience when we realized that we were persecuting Christ by denying our own integrity of sexuality and faith as gay and lesbian and bisexual Christians. Transgender Christians know a similar experience of denial and conversion, as do our families and friends. Of course, along with Saul and Fred, we were misled by our religious backgrounds, our sometimes mistaken religious zeal, and occasionally by psychosocial maladjustment.

Like Saul, we may have been temporarily blinded by such an epiphany, not knowing what to do next. As Saul benefited from Ananias (Acts 9:10–19), we have been blessed with spiritual mentors whose "unblinding light," directly or through their writings, illumine the meaning of our individual epiphanies.

Thank you, God, that we have seen your light in Jesus smiling on us, converting us into kinder, gentler Christians. Thank you for the mentors who help us understand our epiphanies as a call to personal integrity as well as evangelism in our community and the church.

> *Now in Joppa there was a disciple whose name
> was Tabitha, which in Greek is Dorcas. She was
> devoted to good works and acts of charity. At that
> time she became ill and died.* Acts 9:36–37

When Peter came to visit, "all the widows stood beside him,
weeping and showing tunics and other clothing that Dorcas
had made while she was with them" (Acts 9:39).

When my mother died, my brother and sister and I joined
her whole church family to remember her many good works
and acts of charity. What was most valuable to us in her home
were those things that had her touch: her lifelong collection
of pitchers, material she had embroidered, letters and school
lesson plans she had written, books she had read, her cher-
ished maple table and chairs. We have since been caught up
in her "afterlife," that afterglow of her life that is left within
our hearts and minds and souls.

An Asian woman who spoke no English came to her
funeral and let out a heartfelt wail over her coffin. She was a
neighbor whose garden my mother had complimented as
she walked to the store. Thus began a series of exchanges of
flowers from each other's gardens and small, thoughtful gifts
on occasion. The morning of Mom's funeral, the woman left
a bouquet of flowers on Mom's front porch.

"The only thing you take with you is what you give away."
This framed sentiment hangs in George Bailey's office in my
favorite film, *It's a Wonderful Life*. Even before Peter prayed
and Tabitha was raised to new life, her life continued in what
she had given away to other women. And note that she was
referred to as a "disciple."

Thank you for mothers, sisters, daughters, cousins, aunts, grandmothers, lovers, and girlfriends who still live to us as they live to you, Eternal God. Embrace them in your everlasting arms as we hold them in our hearts. We pray, and they come to life!

> *But [Jesus] answered her, "Martha, Martha, you*
> *are worried and distracted by many things; there*
> *is need of only one thing. Mary has chosen the bet-*
> *ter part, which will not be taken away from her."*
> Luke 10:41–42

As a young priest, Henri Nouwen gave beds to a poor family who had been sleeping several to a bed. The family, in turn, sold the beds so they could give a party for their friends. Henri concluded they needed this more. Hospitality requires listening at the feet of our guests to discern what gifts they need and what gifts they offer.

While Martha was trying to be hospitable by her prepa-rations in the kitchen, Mary was trying to be hospitable by sitting at Jesus' feet, engaged in dialogue.

Sometimes we in our community become obsessed with our clean homes, groomed yards, plentiful parties, and ele-gant dinners as a means of hospitality. But we can become so frantic and intense that we may miss the whole point of hos-pitality, which I would say is to *be* with people. Yes, we are providing opportunities for other people to be together while we flutter about tending to everything from enough appetizers to spilled drinks, and that is a great gift. But an absentee host is usually distressing to a guest, and we may miss what a guest is really searching for. Similarly, an over-bearing host ("You *will* enjoy this, won't you?" Or "You will enjoy it my way, not your way!") is intimidating and unwel-coming to any guest, from a partyer to a lover.

This can be true in churches as well. Worship leaders may be so intent on providing the best music, the finest liturgy, and the most thoughtful sermon that we fail to listen to the actual spiritual needs of the congregation, which may simply be to sit and talk about our doubts and lives.

And, in terms of social justice (as well as simple social setting), like Henri Nouwen we sometimes determine what marginalized individuals or communities need without adequate consultation. Just because they may be missing what we have doesn't mean that what we have is what they want.

Just as I anticipate that you, the Lord of hosts, will drop everything to listen to me, your guest in prayer, so may my guests anticipate my attentiveness toward them and their well-being. May my home become home for others, a safe place away from demands of conformity and performance.

> *"And his master commended the dishonest man-*
> *ager because he had acted shrewdly; for the chil-*
> *dren of this age are more shrewd in dealing with*
> *their own generation than are the children of*
> *light."* Jesus, in Luke 16:8

Jesus' dishonest manager would do well on TV's *Survivor*.

We might be a little mystified about Jesus' parable of the dishonest manager who, upon learning he was about to be discharged for mismanagement, cut in half what his master's debtors owed so they would be beholden to him in his unemployment.

Epiphanies are more than inbreaking light from the commonwealth of God. Epiphanies are more than glimpses of the eternal and the sacred, more than insight. Epiphanies are opportunities the shrewd must seize, doorways by which to enter that light or usher others into that light. It is not enough to know the way: one must be *on* the way, one must *become* the way, one must *show* the way.

One of the first things I learned on a church staff was that a pastor doesn't just keep office hours and expect the world to come to him or her. While a minister (and all Christians are ministers) must be accessible, she or he has to go out and search for opportunities to minister, whether within a congregation, a community, a campus, or a movement. One must be shrewd to discern where your gifts and the needs match, as well as just how many concerns you can possibly address. And you must care for your own needs.

Progressive Christians, in my experience, are not very shrewd. We want to address every issue at once, and we end up being less effective, both because we can't possibly do justice to every issue, and because people around us feel bombarded with our many causes. Then we burn out because we have not tended our own gardens. I believe we should leave "fixing the world" to God and the whole people of God. Individuals could then focus on one or two aspects of the whole picture. It rids us of our messianic pretensions, and it trusts others to open doors to God's commonwealth.

Gays and lesbians, bisexuals and transgenders, however, are often too shrewd for our own good. We've struggled to survive, often completely on our own, since, unlike those from most other marginalized groups, our communities, families, friends, and congregations usually have not consisted of our own kind. Thus relationships, teamwork, and coalitions may not come naturally to us; we may even distrust them. Even sharing our spirituality in community is problematic. We are sometimes better at manipulation than mutuality. We should not have been surprised that TV's first "Survivor" was a gay man!

Help us to be shrewd as serpents, yet gentle as doves. We want more than survival. We want to be surrounded by people with whom we've worked for justice, played for fun, loved in mutuality, prayed in community, and lived as family. Amen.

> *God builds up Jerusalem;*
> *   and gathers the outcasts of Israel,*
> *heals the brokenhearted,*
> *   and binds up their wounds,*
> *determines the number of the stars;*
> *   and gives to all of them their names.*
> Psalm 147:2–4

I am struck by the juxtaposition of God's gathering outcasts and naming stars, as if of equal importance in the divine plan. I can't recall ever seeing two such different enterprises so closely linked in the same scripture passage. Doing good and creating beauty are in the same breath and breadth of God; gathering outcasts, healing the brokenhearted, binding wounds, determining the number and names of stars. God is not a specialist.

Some of us have a keen sense of ethics and others of us have a keen sense of aesthetics. We can be judgmental of one another, or we may blend our passions as God does, valuing one another's gifts at determining justice or discerning beauty. Instead of assuming a hierarchy of values, we may share the Psalmist's epiphany that justice and beauty go together in all that is sacred.

God also "builds up Jerusalem"—at the time of the Psalmist, the political and spiritual center of Israel. Thus even politics and spirituality blend together in God's concern for God's people. Some of us want to separate the two. But even in a nation that forswears any "establishment" of an official religion, spirituality as well as politics must be heard in the public square to maintain cultural vitality. (See Stephen Carter's *The Culture of Disbelief* [HarperCollins, 1993].)

Ethics and aesthetics, religion and politics, are all part of the divine mix. If they weren't, how limited our conversations would be—in the church or over dinner!

Bless us in our spiritual quests for justice and beauty, especially in politics and religion! May we see you at work in every corner of our lives, gathering outcasts, healing the brokenhearted, binding wounds, and making stars.

> *I appeal to you, sisters and brothers, by the name*
> *of our Lord Jesus Christ, that all of you agree and*
> *that there be no dissensions among you, but that*
> *you be united in the same mind and the same*
> *judgment.* 1 Corinthians 1:10

Well, that ain't gonna happen. Not in the gay community. Not in the church.

But it's refreshing to realize that division was evident in the earliest of church writings, Paul's letters. The later-written Acts of the Apostles had it that the early Christians were all of "one heart and soul, and ...everything they owned was held in common" (Acts 4:32). But I've wondered if this retrospective depiction is the way things *should* have been in the early church rather than the way things actually *were.*

Even the story of Pentecost has struck me as an idyllic dream of the way the church *should* have begun—a dramatic turnaround, an inpouring of the Spirit that empowered early Christians to proclaim the gospel in the languages of strangers so the message could be taken all over the world. Maybe it gives today's church, so divided by language, culture, and belief, an impossible ideal.

"For it has been reported to me by Chloe's people that there is quarreling among you, my friends. What I mean is that each one of you says, 'I belong to Paul,' or 'I belong to Apollos,' or 'I belong to Cephas,' or 'I belong to Christ.' Has Christ been divided?" Paul asks rhetorically (1 Corinthians 1:11–13). Sounds like a political convention! Or a queer activist strategy session! Or a church assembly!

We should be glad for division and disagreement in

whatever setting. It reveals God's restless Spirit at work. It marks the difference between a movement and fascism, between a church and a cult.

Thank you, God, for our divisions. They liven things up, and make us realize that we are alive, not yet "resting in peace." Thank you that we have beliefs, that we have passions, that we care enough to struggle. May our belief and passion and care for one another keep us together while we struggle for one another's blessings—as well as yours!

FEBRUARY 10

> *Jesus went throughout Galilee, teaching in their*
> *synagogues and proclaiming the good news of*
> *the kingdom and curing every disease and every*
> *sickness among the people.* Matthew 4:23

Amanda Udis-Kessler is a wonderful writer who has contributed to *Open Hands*, a magazine I edit for congregations welcoming of LGBT folk. She wrote an article about Jesus that prompted me to observe that she, a Unitarian Universalist, seemed closer to Jesus than most Christians who wrote for the publication! She explained that Jesus was her primary spiritual authority.

Jesus is my primary spiritual authority as well. Like Amanda, I don't know what to make of all the theological and doctrinal and confessional explanations under which the person of Jesus seems buried once again. I do know that I trust Jesus in a way I would never trust a theologian or teacher or leader of the church.

That is not to say Jesus would be easy for me to be with. He would challenge many of my beliefs and behaviors, yet I would know that his challenges would not be to control or make me conform, but to assist me in my growth. And I believe it would be just plain wonderful to be alongside him, sensually and spiritually. His charisma, his wisdom, his love would capture me, and I'd become some lovesick disciple like the beloved disciple John.

That does not mean that I would not desert, betray, or deny him when the going got tough. I can claim no moral superiority to Judas or Peter or the other disciples. I have seen myself betray or deny or abandon Jesus in my own life in less dire circumstances than they faced with him.

Yet more than any other human being that ever existed, Jesus best represents to me who God is. His life was an ongoing epiphany—what it meant to be God's beloved, to be Messiah, to be human, to be divine.

This scripture from Matthew makes me feel nostalgic for what might have been, if only.... Or what might be, if only I would fully commit myself as his disciple.

Jesus, you are my friend and I sincerely want to be yours. May I be present to you as you are present to me. May I fully embrace your presence, as you fully embrace mine. May I allow you to touch me, hold me, kiss me, and teach me.

> *God has told you, O mortal, what is good;*
>   *and what does the LORD require of you*
> *but to do justice, and to love kindness,*
>   *and to walk humbly with your God?*
> Micah 6:8

It's so simple. Why don't we just do this?

Because doing justice means giving up privileges, reforming institutions, changing our ways. Because loving kindness means forgiving others, being gentle when we feel fierce, not shaming but upbuilding people. And walking humbly means not insisting on our own way, seeking dialogue and mutuality and consensus, listening to others as well as to God. Already we should feel exhausted.

Yet notice what is not listed: all those things we normally associate with religion—worship, belief, membership. Micah states God's requirements after rhetorically asking what kind of ritual sacrifice God wants. God requires more than *ritual* sacrifice, he concludes. God requires the sacrifices entailed in doing justice, loving kindness, and walking humbly.

Micah probably assumes that the other stuff of religion is to be done, as both support and prod for doing what God requires, but *not as a substitute*. Worshiping a righteous God reveals justice as a divine activity. Believing in a merciful God unveils kindness as sacred. And membership in a spiritual community keeps us humble.

Worship, belief, and belonging make *us* feel good.

Justice, kindness, and humility make *everyone* feel better.

Righteous God, may our worship lead to justice. Merciful God, may our beliefs generate kindness. Welcoming God, may our belonging to the family of faith keep us humble.

> *And in the morning, a great while before day,*
> *Jesus rose and went out to a lonely place, and*
> *there Jesus prayed.* Mark 1:35

Millions of neutrinos pass through the atoms of our bodies every day. These particles are emitted by the sun's nuclear activity, and were theorized twenty years before their existence could be demonstrated in a lab, so difficult are they to discern.

I believe epiphanies are like neutrinos. Every day, millions pass by us—sometimes through us—but we detect only a few. They are emitted by God's divine activities, and have kept the spiritual quest alive in the human race for generations without having been proven in any laboratory. (Though many epiphanies have happened in laboratories!)

A time of prayer and meditation gives us a window of opportunity to discern epiphanies in our lives. Like Native American dream catchers, providing ourselves with space and time and material for "catching ourselves" in reflection helps us notice the instances when God or the sacred is revealed to us.

The space might be a cathedral or our favorite chair. The time may be early in the morning, like Jesus, or in the middle of our workday. The material may range from a lit candle to scriptural or devotional material.

Jesus chose a lonely place devoid of people needing his attention. He had spent the day before healing all kinds of people in the city and this day "everyone is searching" for him. Jesus chose to go to the lonely place "a great while before day," when the wondrous stars were out and he could watch the magnificence of sunrise awakening the world. His materials for meditation were his own words to God.

Albert Einstein said, "There are only two ways to live your life. One is as though nothing is a miracle. The other is as though everything is a miracle." Miracles are just another way of describing epiphanies.

Help me to find the words to catch my life as it flows by! Bring to mind all the ways you may have touched me with your holy presence in recent days. The aroma of that flower. The laughter of that child. The breeze on my sweaty brow. That feeling of being loved. That acknowledgment of my efforts. That scripture that speaks so deeply to me. The touch of my pet. That idea I had yesterday. Thank you, thank you, thank you!

FEBRUARY 13

"Remember that my life is a breath." Job 7:7

Life is short and tough and then you die.

For my fiftieth birthday, my friends George Lynch and Louie Tamantini gave me a big blowout party in their home in Long Beach, California. I visited my parents' graves on my birthday, thanking them for my fifty years of life. And I made my funeral arrangements.

It was not a morbid thing to do. It was a rite of passage. My reading for the trip to California was Mardi Tindal's *Soul Maps: A Guide to the Mid-life Spirit* (United Church [of Canada] Publishing House, 2000). In it, midlifers acknowledged ritual as an appropriate marking of their transitions.

Making my funeral arrangements was acknowledging that I am going to die. Even the people at the mortuary, which encourages such prearrangements, seemed surprised to see me. I enjoyed "lightening up" the serious representative who helped me, who turned out to be very gay-friendly. Considering a coffin with a pink lining, I questioned whether the color was intended for men. He said he thought it would set my skin off well. He held the material up to my face, and I joked, "So you think I can pull this color off?"

I selected a coffin that seemed very European (once a queen, always a queen!) and inexpensive (once a frugal Presbyterian, always . . .). I leaned into it, sniffed, and said, "Ah— that new–coffin smell!"

Once upon a time I had intended to be cremated, with my ashes strewn at a site above Mount Calvary Retreat House in Santa Barbara. But when my mom, who opposed my cremation, died, I decided I wanted to be buried with my family.

Though I'm not certain what lies beyond, I do not think my death will be the end of me. God loves us eternally, I am sure. What form that love and life will take is up to God. For what has been and what will be, my marker will read, "Thanks, God!"

I trust you, God. You've given me more life than I expected when my eyes first looked beyond my baby blanket. It just kept expanding and expanding. More people loved me than I anticipated in my lonely adolescence. I've been to more places than I dreamed. I've had the opportunity to give my life and my writing to a good cause. Thanks, God!

> *God is love, and those who abide in love abide in*
> *God, and God abides in them....There is no fear*
> *in love, but perfect love cast out fear; for fear has*
> *to do with punishment, and whoever fears has*
> *not reached perfection in love. We love because*
> *God first loved us.* 1 John 4:16, 18–19

Realizing that "God first loved us" is an epiphany. That is to say, it must be experienced. One may argue it. One may reason to it. One may imagine it. One may even believe it. But epiphanies are more than argument, reason, imagination, and belief. Epiphanies are experiences.

Consider your history and you may find more experiences of God's supposed "un-love" than of God's love: A scripture passage condemning who you are. A sermon attacking gay rights. A family member rejecting you for religious reasons. A beloved church friend pulling away because of your self-disclosure. A person refused membership in your church for being gay. Denominations refusing ordination of gays and lesbians. Religious groups and leaders pressuring legislatures to allow only heterosexual marriage. Attending a heterosexual marriage in a church that would never bless your relationship.

Now read your love letters from God: A scripture passage that moved you because it defended someone who was oppressed. A sermon that touched you for being so welcoming. A family member who embraced you because "that's what Christ would do." A beloved church friend who hugged you when you came out. A church that openly welcomes lesbians and gay men, bisexuals and transgenders.

Denominations that ordain us. Religious groups and leaders pushing for gay marriage. Attending a same-gender marriage in an inclusive church.

Maybe your love letters from God were a little different than these. Maybe you haven't received all your love letters from God—but I promise you, they're on the way.

As we grow in our experience that God first loved us, we can see the imperfection in those people and churches that fear us. We can see our own imperfection in fearing them or God. We can understand that those who love us abide in God and God in them. We can understand that we abide in God because we love. And we experience that God is love.

Oh happy day! When you first loved me as a twinkle in my parents' eyes, knit me together in my mother's womb, awesomely, wonderfully made in your image—who am I that you are mindful of me, O God? And yet you first loved me, and so I love. Thanks be to you, divine Lover!

> *Last of all, as to one untimely born, Christ appeared also to me. For I am the least of the apostles, unfit to be called an apostle, because I persecuted the church of God. But by the grace of God I am what I am, and God's grace toward me has not been in vain. On the contrary, I worked harder than any of them—though it was not I, but the grace of God which is with me.* 1 Corinthians 15:8–10

Those of us who are gay men might empathize with Paul. He was the last chosen for Christ's team. Those of us who were the last picked when gym class divided into teams know what that's like. Each of us was the doofus that the captain and teammates didn't trust to play well enough to help the team win.

Paul was the last chosen by captain Christ for the apostle team. His teammates wouldn't trust him for a very long time because he had played for the other team, so to speak, as a zealous Jew who thought that Christians were heretics. But, thanks to God's grace and Paul's own hard work, he became a respected team player. Gay men may not have done that on the playing field, but we certainly overachieved when it came to the arts and academics.

Lesbian girls were often the first chosen for their teams in gym class. They seemed to love sports and had the agility and ability and ardor to carry it off. But when it came to what team they played on sexually, homosexuality seemed to choose them later than the gay boys. Most of us, whether lesbian, gay, or transgender, tried unsuccessfully to make it on the other team. And though bisexuals could make it on either team, they were often welcome only if they could "pass" as an "authentic" member of one or the other team.

No matter when any of us were chosen for the queer team, most gay men and lesbians alike have told me they wished it had happened earlier. So did the apostle Paul—that is, he wished he'd been chosen for the Christian team earlier. He felt he had a lot to prove, joining the team later in the game. Many of us felt we had a lot to prove sexually by the time we joined the gay team.

But we have nothing to prove or apologize for. By God's grace, we are what we are, we came out when we came out, and God's grace toward us has not been in vain.

Thanks for choosing me for the queer team, God. I like our lavender uniforms, our lambda logo, our rainbow flag, our pink triangles, our coed locker rooms.

> *Then Jesus cried again with a loud voice and*
> *breathed his last. At that moment the curtain of*
> *the temple was torn in two, from top to bottom.*
> *The earth shook, and the rocks were split.*
> Matthew 27:50–51

At least, that's what *should* have happened when Jesus died. That's what should happen when *any* of our dear lovers or family members or friends die, let alone the Savior of the world.

I am not going to rise to the occasion of addressing the meaning of this text and its context. For that I would recommend continuing to read this little book through Lent and Holy Week. What I want to focus on is the tearing of the Temple curtain, that which separated the Holy of Holies from the rest of the Temple, from the rest of us. In Christ's death, we now have direct access to the presence of God.

The curtain should remind us of the veil that Moses had to wear over his shining face because it reflected his encounter with God's, *Shekinah*, God's divine glory. It might also remind us of Paul's writing that Christians look into one another's faces unveiled, growing in one another's glow. In that context he pejoratively wrote of the ancient Hebrews that their minds were veiled.

What struck me as I read today's reading is that *all* our minds are veiled to epiphanies of our past, which later experience may tear or shake or split open. Let me explain.

As I write this, my golden Labrador retriever Calvin is curled up underfoot under my desk, his usual place when he is frightened. We were awake a good part of the night because he hurt his back and could not lie down without great pain. We spent part of the night sleeping together on the floor. Hobbes, who usually barks for attention when I give Calvin my affection, did not, and kept looking curiously and sympathetically into Calvin's face.

Earlier in the evening, when I hugged him gently in sympathy, Calvin reflexively bit my hand, for the first time. I understood his defensiveness, but it made me cry. My tears were about more than feeling hurt or being hurt. Recent nightmares have revealed my terror of losing either of my dogs, Calvin or Hobbes. After the great losses of my mother in death and my lover in divorce last year, and a series of lesser losses since, this loss would be the final blow. My feelings have been close to the surface.

This morning I thought of the time in eighth grade at my fundamentalist Christian school when a teacher fainted in front of our class. Later I learned that she had had a nervous breakdown while serving as a missionary to South America. I remembered how emotional she had always been, how frustrated and lost she seemed. This morning the veil fell from my eyes and I understood what she felt. My sympathies poured out for her in a way they never could when I was in her class. I recognized in her as well as in myself something holy. Caring so much, while difficult to hold in earthen vessels, is God's way.

God, thank you for epiphanies that dawn on us even as much as a lifetime later. Thank you for my teacher's vulnerability, her willingness to feel so deeply her love, her doubt, her struggle, her faith, her hope. Thank you, too, for her willingness to come back to the classroom and speak candidly about her apprehensions returning after such a display of vulnerability. Send us all into that mission field, O Lord.

> *Just after daybreak, Jesus stood on the beach; but the disciples did not know that it was Jesus. Jesus said to them, "Children, you have no fish, have you?" They answered, "No." He said to them, "Cast the net to the right side of the boat, and you will find some." So they cast it, and now they were not able to haul it in because there were so many fish.*
> John 21:4-6

It was then that "the disciple whom Jesus loved" recognized the resurrected Lord.

People who fish—who we know tend to love myth, especially in terms of "the one that got away"—might be the first to demythologize this miracle by pointing out that someone standing on the shore might be able to see a school of fish beneath the surface that those right on top of the catch might not see.

This may be used as a parable about epiphanies. Sometimes it takes perspective, either our own over time or that of others in the moment, to catch something sacred. We may be too close to see what lies beneath the surface.

In a parallel story in Luke (5:1-11), before Jesus calls Simon Peter as a disciple, Jesus does the same trick, but without the benefit of perspective. Some people are like that, and especially Jesus. It terrified Peter, who asked him to leave, saying, "I am a sinful man!" (Luke 5:8).

But of course the greater miracle in John's version is the appearance of the resurrected Jesus, whom the disciples did not recognize at first. "The disciple whom Jesus loved" had the perspective of love by which he recognized Jesus. Others who saw him after his crucifixion had the perspective of belief by which they knew him, because the accounts all carefully indicate that the resurrected Christ appeared only to believers.

Perspective, love, and belief all help us see things not otherwise readily accessible.

Bless me with perspective that helps me see beneath the surface, love that helps me recognize true identity, and belief that opens me to possibilities of glory revealed.

> *The heart is devious above all else;*
> *it is perverse—*
> *who can understand it?*
> *I the Lord test the mind*
> *and search the heart,*
> *to give to all according to their ways,*
> *according to the fruit of their doings.*
> Jeremiah 17:9–10

Jeremiah should be the patron saint of curmudgeons.

But he's right. Anyone who's fallen in love with the wrong person knows how deceptive the heart can be.

Yet the heart was not considered the center for romantic feelings when Jeremiah turned this phrase. The heart was the seat of human will. Our wills are devious and perverse, Jeremiah suggests. We deceive ourselves that our will is God's will.

We can't really know God's will, although we may surmise with our spiritual ancestors that God's will is life and love and all those things that bring life and love to others, such as mercy and justice.

But God, Jeremiah claims, can know our will. Surrounding us like an MRI, God probes our minds and hearts for evidence of faithfulness. (Maybe that's where those people who think they've been probed by aliens get the idea!)

Since we can't do that, we need to look at our "ways" and "the fruit of [our] doings." Does the way we live our lives nurture life and foster love in ourselves and others? Do our lives produce the fruits of mercy and justice?

Much of what we do is simply to survive, to sustain life. Taking time to truly nurture life is something else again, from taking time to pray to taking time to play. And much of the "fruit" we produce is simply so we have something to trade with others: for example, I'll give you so much forgiveness for this much forgiveness, and this much justice for this much justice, an eye-for-an-eye, tit-for-tat arrangement. But I think the fruit expected by God is to pour out of us like an overflowing cornucopia.

We must not live small. We must live big. Otherwise there's little in it for us.

O Lord, you have searched me and known me....
You search out my path and my lying down,
and are acquainted with all my ways....
Search me, O God, and know my heart;
test me and know my thoughts.
See if there is any hurtful way in me,
and lead me in the way everlasting. (Psalm 139:1, 3, 23–24)

But as for me, my feet had almost stumbled;
my steps had nearly slipped.
For I was envious of the arrogant;
I saw the prosperity of the wicked.
For they have no pain;
their bodies are sound and sleek.
They are not in trouble as others are;
they are not plagued like other people.
Therefore pride is their necklace....
They scoff and speak with malice....
Therefore the people turn and praise them,
and find no fault in them....
Such are the wicked;
always at ease, they increase in riches.
Psalm 73:2–6, 8, 10, 12

It's easy to believe that some bitter queen sitting in a gay bar or at a gay circuit party wrote this. That, of course, is not what biblical scholars say, but it would explain a lot. "Their bodies are sound and sleek" would translate well in our experience: "Their bodies are buff and smooth and slender." "Pride is their necklace"—everything from Mardi Gras beads to pearls to chains to phosphorescent neckbands. "They scoff and speak with malice" is the ancient Hebrew version of "they have a lot of attitude and they love to gossip." "Always at ease, they increase in riches." Where *do* so many gay guys get so much disposable income to go out so much and afford traveling to all these circuit parties? Wish *I* could find the source! "Therefore the people turn and praise them." More like *envy* them and *want* them.

O.K., so now *I* sound like that bitter queen, but not as poetic as the Psalmist!

The truth is, we don't really know anyone's experience. And homophobia and envy and our own insecurity all may affect our judgment of others. When people in a bar setting say to me they could never find somebody worthwhile there, I remind them that *they themselves* are in the bar and surely *they* are worthwhile! We have to set aside any notion that those in bars or at circuit parties have the wrong priorities. I mean, I see churchgoers in bars and have attended a couple of circuit parties myself!

But the Psalmist does ask a question that is more intriguing to me than "Why do the good suffer?" After all, *everyone* suffers. It is "Why do the wicked prosper?"

I hope you don't expect an answer from me. Much more spiritually vital is how we respond to the wicked prospering: "But as for me, my feet had almost stumbled; my steps had nearly slipped. For I was envious of the arrogant; I saw the prosperity of the wicked." If we let this perceived unfairness get to us, we may lose our own way. Despite the Psalmist's frequent calls for vengeance, we do not find our way to God by trampling on others for their supposed deficiencies. Later in the psalm the writer admits,

> When my soul was embittered,
>   when I was pricked in heart,
> I was stupid and ignorant;
>   I was like a brute beast toward you.
>   (Psalm 73:21–22)

God, save us from our own arrogance and brutishness and envy and bitterness. Bless the buff and smooth and sleek. Bless the party boys and girls. Bless the rest of us. Bless us all with a way to find you and to discern the good and godly. Amen.

> *For the word of the cross is folly to those who are*
> *perishing, but to us who are being saved it is the*
> *power of God.* 1 Corinthians 1:18

That the disciples could see divine glory and salvation in Christ's seemingly senseless, clearly brutal, and movement-destroying crucifixion is most amazing. "Anyone hung on a tree is under God's curse," Deuteronomy 21:23 declares. How could they declare otherwise? And how can we wear crosses around our necks and hang them on our walls? Today's equivalent would be wearing electric chairs as jewelry and hanging lethal injection paraphernalia to decorate our homes. It should make us shudder!

Christians are quick to get to the good part of the story, the resurrection, as if that makes the crucifixion palatable. The resurrection should make the crucifixion look even worse, since it is God's vindication of Jesus in the face of such human evil.

Yet the vulnerability that Jesus offered in his life to the point of martyrdom has somehow served as a reconciling catalyst to restore our relationship with God. That sounds crazy, and church teachers and theologians have tried to make sense of it ever since with all kinds of atonement theories. (For my own view of it, see my book *Coming Out as Sacrament*.)

But Paul was content in this instance to let it seem folly to those who miss the point, and then went on to say that the divine folly didn't stop there, for "God chose what is foolish in the world" (1 Corinthians 1:27) as the first Christians. Lest they should boast, Paul even advises the Corinthians,

"You should become fools so that you may become wise" (3:18), following Paul's example: "We are fools for the sake of Christ" (4:10). Will this foolishness never end?

Mardi Gras and Carnival is a time set aside to celebrate human foolishness before the sobering brick wall of Lent, during which we are reminded of the results of complete human foolishness: ignoring and persecuting and crucifying a Savior. Then we will celebrate *God's* foolishness, which is "wiser than human wisdom, and God's weakness [which] is stronger than human strength" (1:25). God's foolishness is reaching out to us in Jesus even when God knows what we'll do with him.

Thanks for being crazy enough to reach out to us anyway, despite all we've done to turn you away! Thanks too for our own folly—our own crazy willingness to give ourselves to others in love, regardless of consequences. May we never become so serious that we cannot play and play well with others, including you!

> *"If the prophet had commanded you to do some great thing, would you not have done it? How much rather, then, when Elisha says to you, 'Wash, and be clean'?"* 2 Kings 5:13

Naaman, the commander of the army of the king of Syria, had leprosy, and learned of a prophet in Israel who might cure him. He went to Elisha bearing gifts for Israel. Elisha didn't even come out to say, "Hey," but sent a messenger with instructions to bathe in the local Jordan River seven times. Naaman was angry and went off in a snit, but his servants intervened with the words quoted above. Naaman followed the instructions and was cured, and decided to worship the God of Israel from then on.

We too think that the spiritual quest must involve rigorous demands, exotic pilgrimages, many books and gurus, a dramatic life-changing moment. And though the spiritual quest may involve all those things at one time or another, it first begins with the simplest step. Spiritual retreats are big these days—thankfully, since I lead them!—and many who attend anticipate a life-changing experience. But better yet is to create for ourselves daily "retreats" when we may contemplate the many ways God reveals God's self and touches our lives.

To serve God, many of us also think we must slay a dragon or find the Holy Grail or rescue the damsel or prince in distress. And though serving God may involve battling institutional dragons or recovering ancient icons or helping the homeless and marginalized, serving God *begins* with the little things and little moments when we are given opportunities to demonstrate our love for God and neighbor: taking an elderly neighbor to the grocery store, rescuing a stray dog, taking a meal to a shut-in, phoning our mothers and fathers.

When we think of the spiritual quest and serving God only in big terms, we are letting capitalistic and materialistic values (where bigger and more are better) shape our spirituality and service. There are "empire builders" even in ministry and the spiritual life. They are often very good people, but they can also get caught up in themselves and their projects. Like the rich man who will have a hard time getting into heaven, they too may have a hard time letting go of their spiritual wealth to really enjoy the inbreaking commonwealth of God that comes to us in little ways, bit by bit, serendipitously, unearned (no matter how much we pray or serve), if only we make time to witness it.

Dear God, please give me vision, vision to see the everyday opportunities for witnessing you in my life and for serving you and my neighbor. With the vision, give me the will to embrace the opportunities.

FEBRUARY 22

> *"If the prophet had commanded you to do some great thing, would you not have done it? How much rather, then, when Elisha says to you, 'Wash, and be clean'?"* 2 Kings 5:13

No, not a mistake. Seems like this scripture could also apply to our love life. Read yesterday's entry to get the full story behind this quote.

Just as we romanticize the spiritual life and our service to God, we romanticize our love lives. Seems funny to state that as a problem, since "romance" and "love" are frequently equated. Think of George Bailey in *It's a Wonderful Life,* who wants to "lasso the moon" for the woman he will marry. We want to do grand things to demonstrate our love to those whom we are wooing or those whom we have wedded.

Yet, as with the spiritual life, it's the simple things that matter most. And it's the simple things that are remembered most when a lover dies or departs. The banana pancakes, Tater Tot casserole, or double-chocolate fudge brownies—his minimalist repertoire in the kitchen. The way she treated your child from a previous marriage as her own beloved child. The popcorn she used to make for you and the dogs when you watched TV together. The attention to detail when he prepared a formal tea with homemade scones on Sunday afternoons.

We also apply capitalistic and materialistic values (bigger and more is better) to appraising our love life: the size of the home we shared, the number of parties given, how many romantic trips, frequency of sex, how many years together, how many lovers. To state the obvious, quality and quantity can not be equated. A love that lasted a week may have been more soul-building than one that lasted years. Going through several significant relationships may be more fulfilling than staying in one. For others, one relationship may be more fulfilling. Marriages with less sex may be more satisfying (including erotically) than those with much. And so on.

It seems true that they don't make marriages like they used to. My mother and father had fifty-one and a half years together before my father's death. Years after Dad passed, Mom and I were making up her bed when I noticed what I thought was laundry detergent on the bottom sheet. She explained she always sprinkled my father's talcum powder on the mattress pad so that the bed would smell like him! And, I found, she slept with a shirt of his under her pillow and his pajama top under his pillow. She had not washed them because they retained his scent.

No matter how grand our romance, it's the little things we did for love that will be remembered.

In a relationship, keep me mindful of details that show my love in ways that grandiose words or deeds cannot match. Seeking a relationship, open me to little ways in which another offers love. Single, reveal to me the nuances of self-love as well as uncommitted love.

> *A person with leprosy came . . . beseeching Jesus,*
> *and kneeling said to him, "If you will, you can*
> *make me clean." Moved with pity, Jesus reached*
> *out and touched the person, and said, . . . "I will;*
> *be clean."* Mark 1:40–41

In Jesus' day, illness and disability were believed to be the result of sin, thus impure or unclean. Though for the most part we no longer hold this view, there is still, in many of us, a feeling that illness or disability somehow taints us. We are damaged goods. We may even consider ourselves dirty; others may as well. We are less than whole. We are imperfect. And so on.

For many, sex is already "dirty." So when it comes to sexually transmitted diseases, we may feel all the dirtier. Herpes, gonorrhea, syphilis, venereal warts, chlamydia, yeast infections, and AIDS may make us feel like the leper who approached Jesus: "If you will, you can make me clean."

Though we can take precautions to protect ourselves and others from sexually transmitted diseases (STDs), safer sex is just that: safer. There is always risk in physical intimacy, and unless we want to live in a plastic bubble, that's a risk love sometimes calls us to take. And for those infected, another kind of risk is taken by sharing this information with loved ones.

Though Jesus may not "be here for the cure," he may still touch us in this story and persuade us we are clean. You see, touching the leper would have rendered Jesus himself "unclean." Jesus apparently had no regard for the categories of clean and unclean. So in that act of long ago, it dawns on us that to Jesus no one is unclean.

Jesus, if you will, you can make me clean. You can make me understand that I am not dirty, I am not damaged goods, I am not imperfect because of illness or disability. You look deeper than others—you get to the heart of my matter. You look past boundaries that regulate other people's regard. You are moved by what I suffer, and your touch is not withheld.

> *As surely as God is faithful, our word to you has not been Yes and No. For the Son of God, Jesus Christ, whom we preached among you, ...was not Yes and No; but in Christ it is always Yes. For all the promises of God find their Yes in Christ. That is why we utter the Amen through Jesus Christ, to the glory of God.* 2 Corinthians 1:18–20

Self-affirmation gurus and methods, eat your heart out! Christ was there first, giving us the positive affirmation we need to make real changes in our lives. So much of religion focuses on human depravity that it's hard to remember we were made in the image of God. Original sin makes it seem impossible to be good or think of ourselves as good. Shame, which has been used to keep us in line, especially as queer people, humiliates us so completely that we can't even *imagine* ourselves capable of taking responsibility for our own lives. We thus "act out" all the more.

Many of us grew up hearing from the pulpit a perversion of Paul's proclamation to the church at Corinth: "Our word to you has been No. In Christ it is always No. For all the condemnation from God finds its No in Christ. That's why we utter damnation through Jesus Christ."

Jesus came to save the world, not condemn it, according to John 3:17. Yet children and adolescents have to be kept in line, so God was often made out to be a punitive father figure who would whup us when he got back or we died, whichever came first. So all this "in-Christ-it-is-always-yes" stuff sounds like so much liberal gobbledygook. If we heard something like that from a pulpit today, we might say the preacher was softhearted and softheaded.

But this is Paul, not the most relaxed or coolest character in the Bible. Not a party animal. Not a Louise Hay or Marianne Williamson. Old Age rather than New Age. So perhaps we should pay attention. God's word has not been equivocal to us. It has not been Yes and No. It has always been Yes. God's promises of presence, deliverance, and advocacy are positive. All those promises are fulfilled in Christ. That's why we can say, "So be it!" ("amen"), through Jesus, to God's glory. We are called to give new meaning to being Yes-men and Yes-women.

Do you really mean it, God? Do you mean to say Yes to me?
Am I truly made in your image? Am I really good inside?
You believe me capable, able to make something of my life?
Amen and amen!

> *Now the eleven disciples went to Galilee, to the mountain to which Jesus had directed them. When they saw him, they worshiped him; but some doubted.* Matthew 28:16–17

We sometimes beat ourselves up when we doubt the Resurrection, but here were disciples *who were actually there*, and yet "some doubted."

We've all had epiphanies that we have doubted: realizations about ourselves or God or the cosmos that seemed too good to be true. "While in their joy they were disbelieving and still wondering," Jesus offered to eat something to show his disciples he was real in Luke 24:41–43.

We remember that at first the men disciples did not believe the women disciples' story about seeing Jesus, for "these words seemed to them an idle tale, and they did not believe them" (Luke 24:11). We also remember the Gospel of John's story of doubting Thomas demanding, "Unless I see the mark of the nails in his hands, and put my finger in the mark of the nails and my hand in his side, I will not believe" (John 20:25).

We, too, have doubted the visions of others, especially those of the disregarded and disrespected, such as women. We, too, have doubted good news when we've heard it, distrusting those who bring it, demanding to see it ourselves.

The church has doubted our epiphany that our sexuality and spirituality are not irreconcilable—that, after all, our sexuality too is a gift from God, and thus our ministries and marriages are already blessed by God. Jesus has already called us to serve our congregations and our community.

Jesus has already turned water to wine at our same-gender ceremonies.

As Jesus "upbraided [his disciples] for their lack of faith and stubbornness, because they had not believed those who saw him after he had risen" (Mark 16:14), so, I believe, he will upbraid those who reject another's epiphany out of hand.

Lord, we believe, help our unbelief! That we are your beloved children is hard to accept. That we belong to you is overwhelming. That you call us to minister in your name is a stumbling block to the church. That you bless our relationships with all the divine rights and privileges of marriage is blowing people away! Blessed are those who have not seen, and yet believe.

> *I give thanks to God always for you because of
> the grace of God which was given you in Christ
> Jesus, ... so that you are not lacking in any spiri-
> tual gift.* 1 Corinthians 1:4, 7

Grace under pressure. For the most part, that cliché charac-
terizes us and our movement to open the church and the culture to us. Think of it—think how many movements in the
world do not have their terrorist components threatening
violence toward other human beings to get their way. Only
the women's movement and the gay movement have
escaped having terrorist groups coercing the dominant society to accept our points of view. Doesn't that suggest something of our God-given spirit and grace?

In the church, those who oppose us most strongly want
us out of the church—excommunicated, given a metaphorical death sentence. By contrast, our movement in the church
has never called for the excommunication of our opponents.
Doesn't this suggest which camp reveals the true Spirit of
Christ?

When we read reports of a shooting or bombing in a gay
bar, a gay-bashing, or antigay threats of violence, I think it's a
wonder we don't return violence for violence. Disgruntled
employees or troubled youths go on a shooting spree to
express their anger and alienation, yet we who have many
reasons for anger and are supposedly the "sick" and "mal-
adjusted" and "militant" ones do not express ourselves violently.

The interfaith organization Soulforce carries out significant demonstrations on our behalf, and much is made of their
"nonviolence." But the fact is, our movement has *always*

been nonviolent. That suggests to me both our health and the rightness of our cause.

Dear God, you have tried to lead us away from false images of you as a god of violence. Keep us faithful to Jesus, the Good Shepherd, the teacher, the vulnerable friend willing to both live and die for his friends. Bless the spiritual gifts we bring to the church and the world, including our love and the peaceful witness of that love. By means of your all-inclusive grace, we pray.

> *While they were eating, Jesus took a loaf of bread,
> and after blessing it he broke it, gave it to the dis-
> ciples, and said, "Take, eat; this is my body." Then
> he took a cup, and after giving thanks he gave it
> to them, saying, "Drink from it, all of you; for this
> is my blood of the covenant, which is poured out
> for many for the forgiveness of sins."* Matthew
> 26:26–28

Yesterday I received a card from "God's glorious gadfly," the
Rev. Howard Warren, retired Presbyterian minister and AIDS
activist and chaplain. It depicted the Last Supper with a car-
toon bubble above one disciple's head, saying, "Bread and
wine? You call that a meal?"

Jesus used the simplest food to convey his greatest hospitality: giving his body and his lifeblood to his friends. In
retrospect, his simple act took on enormous symbolic significance to his disciples, and the reenactment of this sensual
act became a way of telling the story of Jesus. It serves as the
central sacrament of the church that was established in
Jesus' name. A sacrament is a sensual "epiphany," an embodied act that reveals God's presence among us in Jesus Christ.

Babbette's Feast is a wonderful film about a French chef
who serves a Christian sect in the desolate far north of
Europe, an austere group that eschews sensual pleasures.
Their food is very bland until Babbette comes along. She adds
seasoning, which pleases those the sect charitably feeds. Babbette wins a lottery and asks that she be allowed to use her
winnings to prepare the meal that will celebrate the one
hundredth anniversary of the birth of the late founder. The
members of the community are scandalized by the sensual

pleasure of the multiple courses and multiple wine selections. But in the process of the meal, old enmities and divisions within the sect are addressed and overcome. Babbette's feast becomes a healing communion for all.

Our community knows how vital hospitality is. From ordering a pizza for friends to our most elegant and elaborate dinner parties, we provide opportunities for everyone invited to celebrate life through their taste buds and through being at table with others.

Jesus sealed a new covenant between God and us in his final meal with his followers, just as Moses and other leaders sealed the old covenant with God in a holy meal on top of Mount Sinai (Exodus 24:1–2, 9–11). For ancient peoples, "sealing" a covenant transmuted it to an eternal, immutable realm.

In some of Jesus' parables, the fulfillment of God's immutable realm was signified by a banquet to which all are invited, but which some choose not to attend. In every meal that we take the time and attention to appreciate, I believe we may catch a glimpse of the eternal.

May I be attentive to the miracle of the food set before me: the mystery of growth, the stewards of what is grown, those who transport it, those who market it, those who select it and prepare it. Thanks to you and thanks to them, my body can transform their tasty gifts into "sighs, dreams, and laughter," in the words of Zorba the Greek.

FEBRUARY 28

> *Jesus said to them, "Prophets are not without honor except in their own country and in their own house."* Matthew 13:57

Right up front, I'm going to say that I generally do not think of myself more highly than I ought. All of us in the gay movement are prophets, at least to our friends, families, and coworkers. Some of us in the gay Christian movement have had unique opportunities to serve as prophets in our congregations and denominations. And many of us who are Christian, gay or not, have sometimes been a lone voice of faith in secular environments or a lone voice for justice in our churches. It's in this context that I tell the following story.

When we had the final yard sale to empty my mother's house after her death, I suggested to my family that we might say a little prayer in the living room when it was all over, to say goodbye to the house in which we'd all grown up. (If I'd had my druthers, we would have gone from room to room to recount our memories and offer thanks, but I knew my brother and sister would never go for that!)

My brother's response startled me: "What, so you can write about it in your next book? 'We said a little prayer and left the house,'" he mocked, and we laughed together. But I did not bring it up again, and we unceremoniously left the house. It would be my last time inside.

Both my brother and sister may be more mystified by my choosing religion as a profession than by my being gay and a gay activist. With difficulty I had proposed leading us in a prayer at the end of the visitation of my mom's body, a prayer

I was not bold enough to offer at my father's deathbed nine years earlier. All because my siblings know me in a way others do not, and perhaps can't see me as other than their "little brother," the "baby of the family."

"Where did this man get this wisdom and these deeds of power?" people of Jesus' hometown questioned, naming all his family as evidence of his homeliness. "Where then did this man get all this?" (Matthew 13:54, 56). Matthew concludes, "And they took offense at him" (v. 57), and Jesus gave the response about a prophet that is today's text.

Intimacy may get in the way of epiphany, unless we understand that the realm of the spirit is unveiled not by perfect and powerful and faraway people, but by people like us in every way.

And I have the last laugh on my brother, 'cause I got the scene in my "next book" anyway.

God, thank you for the role our mothers and fathers, brothers and sisters, friends and lovers all play in revealing the sacred nature of our lives, shaping our souls and our spirituality in intimate ways, keeping us humble and yet teaching us to be proud. Bless them!

FEBRUARY 29 (*FOR USE IN LEAP YEAR*)

> *Sweet is the sleep of the laborers, whether they eat little or much; but the surfeit of the rich will not let them sleep.* Ecclesiastes 5:12

A commercial for a motel chain cleverly casts a growling Frankenstein and a shrieking Bride of Frankenstein as late-night travelers in need of rest. After a good night's sleep in their motel, the couple climbed back into their car the following morning, looking like an average couple—nothing like the monsters they had been.

Nothing is so underrated in the spiritual life, as well as the whole of life, as sleep. When I started weightlifting in college, I was told there were three important ingredients in body conditioning: sleep, food, and exercise—*in that order*. I think the same is true in spiritual conditioning: sleep, food, and spiritual exercise—*in that order*. (I know some people like to fast and pray, but many who do end up thinking about food rather than faith.)

Sleep deprivation makes us into monsters. Sleep will not make us angels, but will bring us closer to our own ideals as human beings. Countless spiritual guides will tell you that if you fall asleep meditating, that's probably what you need to do and is more important than forcing yourself to stay awake meditating.

Sleep is truly transforming. Countless times have I faced what seemed impossible situations, but then awoke the next morning realizing that with sleep all things are possible, or at least more possible. And "sleeping on it" allows us to give our problems the perspective they need. When I write something, I leave it at least overnight in my computer before sending it to its destination (a reason I don't like sending e-mails!). New ideas and insights may be inserted, as well as changes in words, grammar, tone, and style.

Of course, one may have so many problems or situations ("the surfeit of the rich") that sleep is difficult. But when it comes, if it comes, you know what a difference a night of sleep makes.

"Sleep is the playground of the gods." To state this monothestically, sleep is the playground of God and of God's.

Bless me with a good night's sleep tonight, letting go of the concerns of this day and the troubles of tomorrow. May that divine feeling of falling asleep and being "dead to the world" come upon me, so that I may awake in joy and seize the day!

> *For by grace you have been saved through faith,*
> *and this is not your own doing; it is the gift of*
> *God—not the result of works, so that no one may*
> *boast. For we are what God has made us, created*
> *in Christ Jesus for good works, which God pre-*
> *pared beforehand to be our way of life.* Ephesians
> 2:8–10

Both the Jewish and the Christian concepts of time are linear rather than cyclical, Ecclesiastes notwithstanding ("For everything there is a season . . ."). There is a beginning and an end. Yet certain epiphanies do return again and again, like a comet regularly crossing earth's path in an elliptical orbit. One such epiphany is that life is grace—an unmerited gift from God.

Abraham was saved by faith, as the apostle Paul points out (Romans 4:22), centuries before his people were given the Law of Moses. Paul understands the significance of Christ's life, death, and resurrection as reminding us of the gracious nature of salvation, releasing us from the problematic of adhering to all the rules, as well as delivering us from the presumption and pride that we can earn our salvation by doing so.

Paul quotes Genesis 15:6, "Abraham believed God, and it was reckoned to him as righteousness" (Romans 4:3). In parallel orbit with the epiphany of grace is faith. To believe that life is a gracious gift of God requires faith. To act as if life were a gracious gift of God is the fruit of faith ("created in Christ for good works"). Yet faith itself is a gracious gift of God—to believe in something that gets you out of bed in the morning, that makes you want to live life to its fullest, that prompts you to find meaning, passion, and purpose.

As Halley's comet appears every seventy-six years, so grace appears periodically in the life of the spiritual community to remind it that God's love and our lives are gifts. The periods of Abraham, Christ, and the Reformation are among the times when it came near and shone brightly. May our spiritual community be blessed with yet another such epiphany in regard to our own inclusion in the church.

We need another visit of your grace, dear God. We have fallen into legalism and fundamentalism, believing that we may earn our salvation by our inadequate works and our limited knowledge of you. God, bless us and keep us; may your grace shine upon us and give us peace.

> *"Knowledge" puffs up, but love builds up. If any*
> *imagine that they know something, they do not*
> *yet know as they ought to know. But if one loves*
> *God, one is known by God.* 1 Corinthians 8:1–3

The context of these verses was the early church controversy over whether or not Christians should eat meat from
animals that had been sacrificed to idols. "Stronger" Christians "knew" there was only one God, so such meat had not
been altered by having been devoted to other "gods," and
thus could be eaten without being unfaithful.

But how could those early Christians be so certain that
there was only one God? A recent book (*A World Full of
Gods,* by Keith Hopkins) reminds us that, around the time of
Christ and early Christianity, the Roman Empire played host
to a number of gods and nascent religions. With all these
gods, how did Christians affirm but one? They must have had
doubts!

And that's the point. They must've had doubts. So eating
meat devoted to another god could offend the conscience of
a Christian struggling to believe—the "weaker" Christian,
according to Paul.

The stronger versus weaker Christian analogy has continued to influence Christians' beliefs and behaviors. Thus
those who "know better" are often taught to stifle their freedom to believe and say and do a lot of things "nice" Christians
are not supposed to believe and say and do. After all, we too
live in a world full of gods, idols that distract us from our spiritual focus, and we too live in a church full of Christians less
sure of themselves.

Yet we must remember that the "nice Christian" ideal is also an idol. We must be iconoclastic to the end, that is, ready to break through false or inadequate images of ourselves and of God's expectations of us. "If I partake with thankfulness, why should I be denounced because of that for which I give thanks?" Paul asks on the issue of eating meat offered to idols, something "nice" Christians weren't supposed to do (1 Corinthians 10:30).

At the same time, however, Paul reminds us that "'knowledge' *puffs* up, but love *builds* up" (emphasis mine). Our own pride at being "right" may interfere with the love required to build relationships to the point where full disclosure is possible. Even God didn't reveal God's self all at once, but through a variety of epiphanies throughout scripture, throughout history, and throughout cultures.

Think of the self-righteous "knowledge" of our opponents, which tends to divide rather than upbuild the church. We must not become what we detest. Our love, like all love, is about building relationships—most ultimately with God. "If one loves God, one is known by God." If we love our opponents, they will know us.

God of wisdom—Sophia and Spirit, we understand that the spiritual life is not about having all the answers, but rather about having the passion and the courage to build relationships through which we may discern your presence and your guidance. Bless us in that enterprise.

MARCH 3

> *And God said to me, "You are my servant,*
>   *Israel, in whom I will be glorified....*
> *I will give you as a light to the nations,*
>   *that my salvation may reach to the end*
>   *of the earth."*
> Isaiah 49:3, 6

My, those Israelites thought highly of themselves, to think God would be glorified in them and they would serve as God's epiphany to the nations of the earth!

But maybe the Israelites did not think highly of themselves. In fact, the fuller text shows the "servant" of this second Servant Song in Isaiah to be doubtful of sacred purpose, disclaiming, "I have labored in vain, / I have spent my strength for nothing and vanity" (Isaiah 49:4).

Many of us doubt our sacred worth and that our lives have any sacred purpose. Just as Israel needed Isaiah to remind it of its sacred worth and purpose, so we need to hear our own prophets, who tell us that God will be glorified in us and we will serve as God's epiphany to the church.

Beyond how we "shine" individually, collectively we serve as an epiphany that body and spirit cannot be divided, that one cannot be denied without betraying the other. We manifest the needed integrity and necessary honesty of both sexual and spiritual relationships. We remind the church that, in this life at least, spirituality cannot be disembodied.

How often my spirit has wanted to soar to the heavens in grand and glorious rapture, and my body has seemed to weigh against this! Make me mindful, Body-maker, that all those pleasurable, soaring sensations come from skin, flesh, and brain. What I seek outside my body is within it.

"To the eunuchs who keep my sabbaths,
who choose the things that please me
and hold fast my covenant,
I will give, in my house and within my walls,
a monument and a name
better than sons and daughters, …
And the foreigners who join themselves to
the LORD …
and hold fast my covenant—
these I will bring to my holy mountain,
and make them joyful in my house
of prayer; …
for my house shall be called a house of prayer
for all peoples.…
I will gather others to them
beside those already gathered.
Isaiah 56:4–8

A series of epiphanies in the Bible unveil how broadly inclusive the spiritual community is. In it, the lives of "outcasts"—the excommunicated—are recognized as equally sacred as those "already gathered" in God's family. Eunuchs—by definition non-procreators, and perhaps an occasional euphemism for homosexuals—who choose Yahweh as their God and "hold fast" to God's covenant will have a legacy that goes beyond that of having children. Along with foreigners, they are to be welcomed into God's house of prayer—a direct quote from God, according to the prophet Isaiah.

Jesus would himself quote this passage from Isaiah when clearing an area of the Temple where those other than natural-born Jewish males could gather close to the God of

Israel. And in a teaching that opposed heterosexual divorce, Jesus digressed to say that eunuchs will be in the commonwealth of God. Philip would later interpret Isaiah to the Ethiopian eunuch, who then requested baptism in the name of Jesus.

Traditional requirements of procreative marriage were set aside in the new spiritual community that formed around Jesus and his teaching.

Regardless of sexual orientation, most of our sexual expressions do not enjoy the "justification" of making babies. But that does not mean that they are any less sacred. In truth, recognizing their sacred value enhances our lives and relationships in ways that children cannot.

As we recognize that we are within your "house of prayer" at all times, may even our sexual acts become prayers for intimacy, for mutuality, for pleasure, for re-creation, for play, for union and communion. May our tender caresses become thanksgivings for bodies, for relationship, for covenant with one another and with you. May our lovemaking become sacramental, epiphanies of your presence in the world.

> *A crowd was sitting around [Jesus]; and they said to him, "Your mother and your brothers and sisters are outside, asking for you." And he replied, "Who are my mother and my brothers?" And looking at those who sat around him, he said, "Here are my mother and my brothers! Whoever does the will of God is my brother and sister and mother."* Mark 3:32–35

Another "aha!" about spiritual family. Biological lineage is no longer the criterion for determining one's relationship to the family of faith, or one's relationship to Jesus. "Whoever" does the will of God belongs to Jesus' immediate family. The apostle Peter would have a parallel "aha" in determining that God is not biased, "but in every nation anyone who fears God and does what is right is acceptable to God" (Acts 10:35).

One could broaden the "whoever" and "every nation" to every person along the sexuality or gender spectrum. Regardless of sexual or gender orientation, those who reverence God and do what is right are to be welcomed in the new spiritual community as sister and brother.

Part of my "therapy" in the recent ending of my relationship included watching reruns of the television program *Frasier* while I prepared and ate dinner. First, of course, it made me laugh, even at myself, because the show is about relationships: the difficulty of meeting someone, dating, establishing an ongoing relationship, unhappy relationships, the pain of breaking up. But it all happens to the "singles" in the show, who belong to a nontraditional family: Frasier, his brother Niles, their father and his physical therapist Daphne, the latter of whom both live with Frasier. So, regardless of whatever failures or mishaps occur, they each have a strong base of support to which to return.

Our community has been adept at creating nontraditional families: associations of friends and neighbors, supportive or surrogate family, children from earlier marriages, ours or our partner's, as well as pets, plants, and even stuffed animals! We can remind the church of Jesus' concept that family is truly in the eye of the beholder.

In this era of insular lifestyles, may our churches become the family to which we come home, reminded of our sacred worth, jostled out of ourselves with caring humor, encouraged in our reaching out for intimacy, supported when relationships just don't work out, and challenged to remain open to possibilities.

> *All of them were filled with the Holy Spirit and*
> *began to speak in other languages, as the Spirit*
> *gave them ability. Now there were devout Jews*
> *from every nation under heaven living in*
> *Jerusalem. And at this sound the crowd gathered*
> *and was bewildered, because each one heard*
> *them speaking in the native language of each.*
> Acts 2:4–6

When the Holy Spirit came, the first thing she did was give the disciples the ability to speak other people's languages. The Spirit did not pass an "English only" church law (ludicrous, of course, since the English language wasn't around at the time!). She did not require believers to speak the same language.

A language is more than words. It is culture. A culture expresses itself in how it calls things, how it expresses concepts, how it orders words and builds words, how it conjugates and declines them. A culture expresses itself in the tonality, volume, lilt, and rhythm of its language.

So the early church, in being blessed with the gift of tongues, was given the epiphany of multiculturalism. True, the first believers who spoke different languages were Jews. But, even then, Jews shared one faith but not necessarily one culture. In the same way, Christians would also share one faith but not one culture.

Our community also transcends cultures. We speak in many languages. Even when we share the same culture, we may not share the same language as lesbians, gay men, bisexual women, bisexual men, transgenders (themselves diverse and not of one experience), and our families, friends, and advocates.

We need to pray for the gift of the Holy Spirit—not necessarily requesting the gift of tongues, but rather the gift of ears, so we may be attentive to one another and listen to one another and our unique experiences of faith.

Others have so much to teach me about you, O God. Open my ears, my heart, my mind, and my soul to their insights into you and into human nature. Only from them may I know you more completely, and come to know myself a little better.

MARCH 7 OR LAST DAY OF EPIPHANY, THE TRANSFIGURATION

> *Jesus took with him Peter and John and James,*
> *and went up on the mountain to pray. And while*
> *he was praying, the appearance of his face*
> *changed, and his clothes became dazzling white.*
> Luke 9:28–29

Mardi Gras and Carnival are in full swing in New Orleans and places like Rio, and we are either there or wishing we were! The desire to transfigure our personas (masks) and to play without reservation balances the serious introspection and somber repentance that will come with Lent.

Jesus' visage was transfigured "while he was praying." He was joined in conversation by Moses and Elijah, symbolizing the Law and the Prophets. Peter and John and James were "weighed down with sleep," in that delicious and often visionary state between consciousness and sleeping, and they saw the glory of it all. Enthusiastic and impetuous Peter wanted to build something to contain or commemorate it all. A cloud overshadowed them, and a voice from heaven gave a message similar to Jesus' baptism: "This is my Son, my Chosen; listen to him!" (Luke 9:35).

The Transfiguration, as it is known, is such high drama that some scholars have suggested that this is a displaced resurrection story. It is a most striking epiphany of Jesus' divine nature, revealed only to Jesus' most intimate circle. It is not for everyone, and Jesus tells them not to tell. Notice the "beloved disciple" is one of the inner circle.

But I wonder if we might switch the components of the idea that this is a displaced resurrection story. Could it be that the resurrection stories are themselves displaced epiphanies of Jesus' sacred nature? That maybe some of those magical, mystical moments that are described as happening later occurred during Jesus' lifetime? I don't mean to be heretical or to deny Jesus' resurrection. It's just that it seems that with Jesus, with God, with epiphanies in general, death is an artificial boundary. What is glorious, sacred, divine, and holy is glorious, sacred, divine, and holy on either side of death.

That means we don't have to wait till we're dead to see the glories of God or to be the glory of God. Epiphanies and transfigurations happen to us now, as with Jesus—while in prayer with God, in conversation with the Law and the Prophets, in the company of believers—and we are transformed, and a voice booms from heaven, "This is my child, my chosen."

"Listen to him!" the voice concludes. We must listen to one another, children and chosen of God. If we do, we'll have a better party than Mardi Gras.

Open my eyes that I may see the traces of your divinity in others. Your glory is their glory, their image is your image. "And all of us, with unveiled faces, seeing the glory of the Lord as though reflected in a mirror, are being transformed into the same image from one degree of glory to another; for this comes from the Lord, the Spirit" (2 Corinthians 3:18). Thanks be to God! Hallelujah! Amen!

PART THREE

Reformation
of the Heart

*Meditations for Lent
and Holy Week*

Introduction

Unless we reform ourselves, we cannot hope to reform the church. And in the act of reforming ourselves, we reform the church. Prayer is the place where reformation begins.

We are often busy people, and do not take the time for daily prayer. But if Jesus needed to pray, how much more do we! The first chapter of the Gospel according to Mark reveals Jesus' busyness. No sooner is he baptized than he is tempted by the worldly concerns of mere survival, proving himself, and acquiring power—all of which he resists. Then he calls his disciples, teaches in the synagogue, casts out an unclean spirit, engages in controversy, and heals Simon's mother-in-law. After all this, Mark reports, "That evening, at sundown, they brought to him all who were sick or possessed with demons. And the whole city was gathered around the door" (Mark 1:32–33). He meets everyone's needs, yet "in the morning, while it was still very dark, he got up and went out to a deserted place, and there he prayed" (1:35). Later, in another deserted place, he would feed five thousand people with a mere five loaves and two fish. The deserted place of prayer led to a rich harvest of souls and sustenance for all.

Prayer for many is an additive for meetings, a reaction to crises, and a refueling station. But prayer for the Desert Fathers and Mothers was a place of conversion. As Christianity became trendy in the fourth and fifth centuries c.e. and the Roman emperor Constantine embraced Christianity, hermit monks went into the desert of the Middle East to pray.

According to Thomas Merton in *The Wisdom of the Desert*, these early monastics saw human culture—even a culture newly christened "Christian"—as a "shipwreck" from which each person "had to swim for his life. . . . These were those who believed that to let oneself drift along, passively accepting the tenets and values of what they knew as society, was purely and simply a disaster" (p. 3). Yet, Merton reminds us, their intent was not only to save themselves: "They knew that they were helpless to do any good for others as long as they floundered about in the wreckage. But once they got a foothold on solid ground, things were different. Then they had not only the power but even the obligation to pull the whole world to safety after them" (p. 23).

Henri Nouwen advised his readers in *The Way of the Heart* to shape a desert for themselves in which to pray. We too need a deserted place to be in communion with the God who creates us, blesses us, delivers us, tabernacles with us, leads us, redeems us, sustains us, loves us. Only then can we survive the shipwreck that is the church, broken by unnecessary divisions and exclusions. Once we gain a foothold ourselves as Jesus did in communion with God in prayer, then we may reach our hand to others seeking freedom and reformation.

There are many characteristics and expressions of prayer. In this brief introduction I focus on three that are close to my heart and my experience that have been "traditioned" to me from the Desert Fathers and Mothers through the work of Merton and Nouwen. Prayer is a place of conversion, of solidarity, and of ecstasy.

A Place of Conversion

The desert hermits found short, simple, and repeated prayers the best for descending with their minds into their hearts, that is to say, to pray with their intellect (minds) and their integrity (hearts). The heart was not considered merely the seat of emotions as we think of it, but the integration of all that we are: body, reason, will, emotion, and moral compass. Thus prayers of the heart lead to transformation.

Blind Bartimaeus of Mark 10:46–52 comes to mind as an example of one who offered short, simple prayers. His cry to Jesus was simply, "Jesus, Son of David, have mercy on me!" Though he was told to shut up, he shouted louder, "Son of David, have mercy on me!" When Jesus called him to come near, Bartimaeus was told by others to "take heart" and asked by Jesus what he wished. "My teacher, let me see again"— another short prayer. Jesus told him, "Go; your faith has made you well." Bartimaeus received his sight and followed Jesus "on the way."

Bartimaeus offers us a spiritual path in our loss of spiritual vision and clarity. We cry for mercy from our God. We ask for spiritual discernment. Jesus reminds us that our own faith is a source of healing. We are thus enabled to follow Jesus as people of the Way, what the first Christians were called.

A Place of Solidarity

Henri Nouwen wrote of the minister (and by that, he meant *every* Christian) as *The Wounded Healer*, that is, as one who understands human vulnerability and woundedness because of her or his own wounds. The Letter to the Hebrews describes Jesus as the wounded healer par excellence: "For we do not have a high priest who is unable to sympathize with our weaknesses, but we have one who in every respect has been tested as we are" (Hebrews 4:15). Thus we are encouraged: "Let us therefore approach the throne of grace with boldness, so that we may receive mercy and find grace to help in time of need" (4:16).

Many of us who are lesbian, gay, bisexual, or transgender and many of our allies have been spiritually wounded, spiritually abused, made to feel as if we were not made in the image of God, persuaded that we are not among God's beloved. We are often tempted—to invert Jesus' saying—to give the judgment we have gotten (Matthew 7:2). Like other forms of abuse, those who have been spiritually abused may be tempted to abuse others spiritually.

But when we approach the realm ruled by grace, we begin to experience a healing. As we allow our lover God to touch us ever so gently, we learn how to touch others who have been spiritually wounded, others who have been spiritually abused. Indeed, it's because of this divine encounter that so many of us already serve in ministry with those victimized by the church as well as society. To avoid burnout, we need to return again and again to the Source of all grace and of all love. Our solidarity with others is possible because of God's solidarity (or intimacy) with us.

Prayer as the Place of Ecstasy

Nouwen loved to play with the origin of words. In *Lifesigns—Intimacy, Fecundity, and Ecstasy in Christian Perspective*, he explained that *ecstasy* is derived from words that literally mean "out of stasis." Prayer takes us outside our selves, beyond a static place, releasing us from inertia. This is the profound spiritual joy the hermits and mystics experienced. It did not necessarily include happiness or perceived craziness, though it could include them both. It meant releasing fear and power and competitiveness, becoming detached from all those measures of failure and success that the world employs. This is the poverty of heart the ancients sought, one that allowed mindfulness of others and attentiveness to God.

After the debacle of the 1978 General Assembly, which set the Presbyterian Church's antigay policy for the decades that followed, I climbed a mountain. As I did, I sensed my identities falling off me like unwanted garments. I was no longer Presbyterian. I was no longer Christian. I was no longer gay. I was no longer male. At the top of my ascent I found an aspen-lined meadow, a sanctuary of beauty where I literally jumped and danced for joy. I had not "arrived," since the top of the mountain still rose above me. But I had let go of much grief and anger and debilitating fatigue, ready to move on. I felt my belovedness in God's realm.

"O taste and see that God is good; / happy are those who take refuge in God," the Psalmist cries (Psalm 34:8) at the end of a litany of praising, seeking, and trusting God. Prayer *moves* us. That's ecstasy.

Conclusion

Lent in particular is an invitation to pray, as Jesus did during his forty days in the wilderness: to be attentive to God's word, to trust God, to worship God alone. The meditations that follow are intended to serve as an invitation to you to find your own words, silences, and acts of prayer during this sacred time.

During a retreat on Henri Nouwen which I led at Kirkridge Retreat Center in Pennsylvania, a woman who is a physical therapist pointed out that "a wound must heal from the inside out." During a similar retreat at Ghost Ranch in New Mexico, a ceramic artist told us that the shape of the inside of a bowl on a potter's wheel determines the shape of the outside.

Prayer is an invitation to reform our hearts even as we call our church to a new reformation. Prayer heals our wounds from the inside out, and shapes us inwardly to determine the form of the church outwardly. Prayer welcomes God as Creator, Jesus as Healer, and the Spirit as Reformer of both our hearts and our church.

The section that follows utilizes the Inclusive Language Lectionary based on the RSV.

ASH WEDNESDAY

> *"Rend your hearts and not your garments."*
> Joel 2:13

"We are so damn proud of our humility!" The mother of my childhood best friend said this, though not to me. She had muttered it under her breath at church one Sunday in my mother's presence, and my mother mentioned it approvingly in a family conversation. I've forgotten the context, but there are so many churchly occasions for which it would be appropriate that it doesn't really matter.

Today many of us will attend, even lead, Ash Wednesday services. Pious sentiment will be running high, a flash flood in the spiritual desert. It will make us feel good to feel so humble. Some of us will have the opportunity to proudly display ashes on our foreheads. People will speak in hushed, gloomy, somber tones as clear evidence of their reverence. Oh, how godly we will be!

I wonder if a more godly sign of penitence for Christians might be to rip up and burn our books of church polity. It could be a way of saying that, as useful an instrument as each may be, they are merely a human attempt to order God's grace, which spills all over the place like rain and sunlight on the just and the unjust.

Some of us will respond that church rules and laws are good things, they just need reforming. I would think the prophet Joel considered the heart a good thing, too, but he heard God calling us to rend it, to tear it asunder, to demonstrate our repentance. Rending church polities might remind us that we need to repent of our *order* that has denied the supposed *disorderly* access to Jesus. Jesus didn't get along too well with the religious lawyers of his day, who brokered the grace of God according to their own polity, the Law of Moses.

May your grace surprise us with its resistance to pride and prejudice.

THURSDAY AFTER ASH WEDNESDAY

Restore to me the joy of your salvation.
Psalm 51:12

We are often better at attending to the *duties* of our salvation. It's part of our heritage, whether as Catholics or Protestants. Our personal salvation is subordinate to the salvation of the world, the transformation needed by which all may share the commonwealth of God. That's why Lent is such a good time for Christians. It justifies our frequently somber preoccupation with everyone else's salvation, whether it's the church conservative's concern for the soul of the church or the church liberal's concern for the soul of society. Nothing's wrong with these concerns, but they distract us from plucking out the two-by-four that blocks introspection.

Many who pick up this meditation book will not have made it to this season. Fewer still will make it all the way to Holy Week and Easter. Though my clumsy and debatable insights will prevent some from continuing, for many it will just come down to a resistance to devoting time to introspection.

But we can't look to God to restore the joy of our salvation if we don't look within ourselves and our schedules to make time to consider our cause for joy. In *Surprised by Joy*, C.S. Lewis tells the story of his wife ignoring a nagging feeling that God wanted her to do something. When she gave in to prayer, she understood God was not calling her to some unattended duty, but to enter into joy.

This time of Lent could be an opportunity to let go of our own plans for the salvation of the church and world, at least for a time, and reflect on the wonder and joy that God would save *us*.

Why me, O God? You surprise me with your saving love! Thank you!

FRIDAY AFTER ASH WEDNESDAY

We are treated as … having nothing, and yet pos-sessing everything. 2 Corinthians 6:8–10

The apostle Paul's lament may be our own. We are treated as if we have nothing to offer the church, and yet we possess everything. We have been given the gospel, an inheritance we share with the church and the world. We have been given the church, though parts of the church and parts of our gay community do not know it yet. We have been given a calling, though confirmed only by welcoming churches.

Being "in" but not "of" the church has given us what those among the "in" crowd don't have: an outsider's perspective. It is from the outside that we may better discern what's missing in the church: integrity of sexuality and spirituality; honesty in all relationships, not just sexual ones; and, of course, a multitude of people.

Often we forget we have everything already. We do not *need* the institutional church. We *are* the church. As Paul would later say of the other apostles regarding their confirmation of his call seventeen years after the fact (Galatians 1:18; 2:1–6), the institutional church will add nothing to us or to the calling we are already fulfilling. In fact, our full acceptance may lose us the invaluable resource of an outsider's perspective. Hopefully, when that happens, we'll listen to other outcasts.

From Hebrew prophets to Jesus, desert monastics to present-day outsiders, may our hearts receive offerings of perspective and prayer.

SATURDAY AFTER ASH WEDNESDAY

"For where your treasure is, there your heart will be also." Matthew 6:21

If we limit our vision merely to what's achievable rather than to full justice, then we begin and end compromised. We will be satisfied with the crumbs that fall from our Master's table. Or, if we finally get "our place at the table" we may be complacent to receive simply *our* piece of the pie rather than struggle on behalf of others.

Many in our community or our churches who preach "gradualism" confuse strategy with goal. "Gradualism" happens only when those impassioned for justice push for full justice, the goal.

We need to learn how to negotiate. In a market in the Middle East, a seller offers an inflated price, a buyer a deflated price, until they settle closer to an agreed-upon worth of the item of purchase. In labor contract negotiations, unions know to ask for more than they expect from an employer so they have a fallback position that is satisfactory.

Our heart must be set on all that we expect of the church, not merely what we think the church will offer at this time.

Make us wise as serpents, while gentle as doves.

FIRST SUNDAY IN LENT

> *"You shall rejoice in all the good which the Sovereign your God has given to you."* Deuteronomy 26:11

Sundays in Lent are set apart from the forty-day fasting period because Sunday was the day of Jesus' Resurrection, thus always an occasion for celebrating his presence among us. So this scripture is appropriate.

Of late my personal prayer life has been characterized mostly by thanksgiving. Instead of praying for people, I thank God for them. And I include those who have died. In place of praying for things like home, family, neighborhood, church, work, relationships, and dogs, I thank God for them. This shift has appeared spontaneous to me, but perhaps it's the Spirit inspiring some new and fresh way to think of prayer. We all have much to be thankful for, if only we take the time to consider "all the good which the Sovereign our God has given [us]."

What's particularly puzzling is that I sometimes even thank God for our opposition, though not for their opposition. (After all, don't *they* tell us they hate the sin but love the sinner?!) This may very well sound patronizing, but I have come to genuinely *feel* for them and their distress. What's going on in their lives that they feel such need to be so rigid when it comes to our acceptance? I think if only we could laugh together, give thanks together, that our opposition would relax and relish a God gracious enough to love even those with whom they disagree.

Our opposition might say the same of us, but our positions are not equal. When we relax with them, we're kicked out of the church. When they relax with us, all of us will be able to stay in the church. It's easy to guess which Jesus would prefer.

Thank you, God, for all you've given to me.

MONDAY, FIRST WEEK OF LENT

Whoever clings to me in love, I will deliver.
Psalm 91:14

Psychologists tell us we're not to cling in love and to avoid those who do. That fits well with our American individualism, which tells us each person must find fulfillment separately on her or his own terms. But I wonder if it's true.

There's some element of clinging in every love. We want someone to need us, to want us around, to hang on our words, to feel what we feel. And when we love, most of us find in the expression of that love elements of needing, wanting, hanging, feeling. Some, wanting to maintain a declaration of independence, call that "interdependence," continuing the myth that we are each autonomous, self-sufficient, and separate beings. Yet even science tells us that we are constantly exchanging subatomic particles with one another!

I don't believe that we're ever separate from those we love. They are always part of us; we are always part of them.

I doubt we're even separate from those who oppose us. They are a part of us, and we of them. They want us to feel their way; we want them to feel our way. Even in opposition, we cling to each other.

Funny that God should want us to cling to her, to him. Why should God need us? Maybe to acknowledge that we can't make it alone—look, we haven't thus far: our very creation occurred because of God's initiative. Our Creator wants to be needed, wants us to hang around, hanging on every divine word, feeling divine feelings of love and compassion. That delivers us from thinking of ourselves as islands.

I cling to you, O God, with all my heart and soul and mind; and I cling to my neighbor as myself.

TUESDAY, FIRST WEEK OF LENT

The scripture says, "No one who believes in Jesus will be put to shame." Romans 10:11

It struck me odd that Paul would be quoting an ancient scripture passage that would specifically name Jesus. His scriptures were Hebrew texts. So I checked it out, and here the Inclusive Language Lectionary rather boldly inserts "Jesus" for "him," presumably originally intended as a reference to God.

I also looked up the allusion, and the NRSV translates Isaiah 28:16 as: "See, I am laying in Zion a foundation stone, / a tested stone, / a precious cornerstone, a sure foundation: / 'One who trusts will not panic.'" Quite a different translation from what the apostle Paul uses!

Our opposition claims that we are "revisioning" scripture in our attempt to gain acceptance. Wasn't that exactly what Christians did from earliest times, illustrated here by the apostle Paul? And what's wrong with bringing a little vision to biblical interpretation?

Our opposition claims that gay priests and gay marriage are never mentioned in scripture. Well, in Paul's day Jesus wasn't mentioned in scripture either, yet early Christians found all kinds of scriptural reasons for preaching his acceptance! Recently I heard a woman mock our opposition's scriptural viewpoint by saying that they seemed to require her own name be personally mentioned in scripture to justify her existence!

We who believe in Jesus will never be put to shame. Paul affirmed this and then proceeded in the next verse to say, "For there is no distinction between straight and gay." At least, that's how I read it in my Bible. Those who trust God will not panic at such an understanding.

Open our hearts to the Spirit's wildly inclusive imagination!

WEDNESDAY, FIRST WEEK OF LENT

And the devil, having ended every temptation, departed from Jesus until an opportune time.
Luke 4:13

Nikos Kazantzakis's *The Last Temptation of Christ* takes its premise from this verse. In the book, the opportune time came at the crucifixion, when the temptation was to lead a "normal" life like everyone else's.

I remember my own temptation to lead a normal life. Get married, have children, take a job like my dad's, delivering bread, live in the suburbs. Most people wouldn't think this an evil temptation, let alone one offered by the devil. Sounds to most people responsible, levelheaded, and generous. And it surely is. I'm grateful my mom and dad made these choices, giving me and my sister and brother a stable home life.

But the Spirit didn't lead me there. One person's temptation is another's calling. One person's calling is another's temptation.

The Spirit led Jesus into the wilderness where he would be tempted. The temptations honed his discernment of the nature of his own calling: it wasn't simply to survive, to control things, or even to prove himself or God. It was to feed on God's word, to worship God alone, and to trust rather than test God. How Jesus worked that out in practical terms was by praying, teaching, healing, rebuking the self-righteous, and comforting the spiritually abused.

The final temptation perhaps was one of compromise. If Jesus had compromised with religious and political authorities, he could have lived a long life, enjoyed the respect of his peers, been given accolades for his service.

But then we probably would not be thinking about him today.

May I follow you, Jesus, into the wilderness to discern your call to me each day.

THURSDAY, FIRST WEEK OF LENT

> *"Look toward heaven, and number the stars....So shall your descendants be."* Genesis 15:5

God said this to Abram, whose faith is "reckoned . . . to him as righteousness" one verse later.

Our descendants will also be innumerable, those whose lives we will make a little easier by modeling to them and to an unfriendly church and culture what it means to be lesbian, gay, bisexual, and transgender.

Abraham and Sarah's descendants, however, have never had an easy time of it. Neither will ours. In many ways it's just as difficult to come out as a youth today as it was twenty years ago. That's why programs are needed for our young people.

Homes are also needed for them—*our* homes—places of occasional retreat from pressure: emotional, spiritual, sexual. The more we can open our homes and our hearts without expectations to lesbian, gay, bisexual, transgender, and questioning youth and young adults, the more blessed our future generations will be.

May we bless our children with safety, support, and spirit.

FRIDAY, FIRST WEEK OF LENT

> *One thing I asked of the LORD ..., to behold the beauty of the LORD.* Psalm 27:4

What does it mean to behold the beauty of God? That's one of those questions which, if you have to ask it, there's no answering it.

Most of us could list limitless instances: love in a lover's eyes, the blooming of an iris, a reflection of trees in a still, crystal lake, stroking the fur of a favorite pet.

But there is beauty that is not so obvious: the frail smile of one who is dying, the job whose loss set us in another direction, the bus we missed so we had a delightful walk, the conversation with a stranger while enduring an interminable wait.

Though verse 4 of Psalm 27 seems to place the beauty of the Lord in God's house, the Psalmist clearly has the bigger picture of God's cosmos at heart. The beauty of God can no more be limited to a church than our beauty can be limited to a closet.

May I behold your beauty, God—just that, just that!

> *Brothers and sisters, join in imitating me.* Philippians 3:17

Arrogance knows no bounds! How can Paul or any but Christ suggest we imitate them? Yet, if we look at the verses prior to Paul's admonition, we discover that the apostle explains he has not yet reached his goal of imitating Christ, but "forgetting what lies behind and straining forward to what lies ahead, I press on toward the goal for the prize of the upward call of God in Christ Jesus" (Philippians 3:13–14). This is what we are to imitate, this pressing on.

Seems to me we too often look around to check out others' imitations of Christ, to make sure they're doing it right, rather than straining forward ourselves.

Our opposition wants to make sure we're all running *straight* (as if we even know which way Christ ran in matters of sexuality!). Our uptight friends want to make sure we're all running "normal," not being "too gay"—whatever that means. Our politically active friends want to make sure we're all out and running to every rally and march.

In our pressing ahead we often look back, living out of past hurts and wounds and mistakes and failures. As a runner, I know that looking back rather than where I'm going may mean more hurts and wounds, mistakes and failures. It's more helpful to *remember* what we've learned from our mistakes as we press forward than to *relive* them, obsessing on what's behind us.

Leaving behind failures and successes, I press on toward the upward call of God in Christ Jesus.

SECOND SUNDAY IN LENT

> *"You will not see me until you say, 'Blessed is the one who comes in the name of the Lord!'"* Luke 13:35

Jesus says this in the context of the way prophets, including himself, are usually treated.

Mother Teresa spoke of "the least of these" with whom she worked as "Christ in a distressing disguise." Jesus said in Matthew 25:31–46 that the righteous would care for him in the hungry, the thirsty, the stranger, the naked, the sick, and the prisoner.

Christ has more masks than the gay community on Halloween! Who was that masked man? Probably Christ.

You might think you know where I'm headed. The church doesn't see that *we* are Christ. But we already know that. The more dangerous question is, Whom don't *we* see as Christ? Men? Women? Transgenders? Bisexuals? Our opposition?

The Hindus use the greeting "*Namustai*," which means "The sacred in me greets the sacred in you." Maybe we could have much more meaningful dialogue with those we would similarly greet with "Blessed are you who come in the name of the Lord." Let's begin every worship and workshop, every conversation and conference by greeting one another in this way. Then maybe the commonwealth of God will feel a little closer and possible.

Blessed am I who come in the name of the Lord. Blessed are you who come in the name of the Lord.

MONDAY, SECOND WEEK OF LENT

> *"Master, it is well that we are here; let us make three booths, one for you and one for Moses and one for Elijah."* Luke 9:33

Peter says this just after he and John and James witness the transfiguration, a mountaintop experience in which the divinity of Christ is revealed through his glow-in-the-dark appearance and his association with Moses the lawgiver and Elijah the prophet par excellence, not to mention the booming voice of God.

Seems like a stupid thing for Peter to say. But then, what is there to say in such awesome company?

Yet it serves as a useful metaphor of how we try to box up and box in the sacred in our midst, especially God. We want to hold on to God, to place limits on God, to keep God boxed in convenient units—dogma, churches, laws, and so on—to keep God in the closet.

And we want to keep boxed up the *imago dei*, the image of God, within us, too—stay in the closet as a beloved gay child of God in the church and in the gay community.

The sacred is one more victim of overpackaging.

Unwrap me, God, so other Christians and other gay people can see my sacred glow.

TUESDAY, SECOND WEEK OF LENT

> *And Moses said, "I will turn aside and see this*
> *great sight, why the bush is not burnt."* Exodus 3:3

Seems curious to me that Moses wouldn't have turned aside to see *any* bush on fire in the wilderness, whether it was being consumed or not. Surely a burning bush would have been unusual, way out in the middle of nowhere!

But it gets me to thinking about those who are "burning bushes" for the church. Much talk these days among do-gooders about "burnout." Maybe there's a lesson here. Moses' curiosity was piqued because the bush was *not* a victim of burnout. Doesn't that suggest that today's human "burning bushes" might do well to work on their stamina rather than their drama, sustaining their spirit while illumining the path for others?

Before I came out, I overdramatized in my mind what people's reaction would be. Though a difficult process with many disappointments, it turned out to be a tremendous relief to come out and receive unexpected support from my family, friends, and the congregations where I had my membership and where I had worked as youth minister.

And though I became, with others, the cause célèbre of the late '70s as one of the openly gay and lesbian candidates for ordination, the energy from that external spotlight needed to be transmuted into an enduring flame carried within us when the media, the public, and the church turned to other concerns. Those unable to carry a torch for the church, so to speak, were enveloped by the darkness of inattention like so many falling stars. Those able to keep their lamps burning in the shadows of the church, like the five wise young women of Jesus' parable, have provided more light over the long run.

Give me oil in my lamp! Keep it burning till the break of day.

WEDNESDAY, SECOND WEEK OF LENT

> *For my thoughts are not your thoughts,*
> *nor are your ways my ways, says the LORD.*
> Isaiah 55:8

God, through the prophet Isaiah, has the audacity to go on to say that God's thoughts and ways are higher than ours! How dare God put us in our place!

I guess it's fair, though. We've been putting God in our place for a long time. Domesticating God, like a pet. God is our buddy, Jesus as our brother—oh, how egalitarian we've become at God's expense and our elevation! In some ways, those things are true. But like any buddy or sibling, there's an unknowable mystery within the persona of God. And unlike any buddy or sibling, God's far beyond our capacity to know, even if God were fully revealed.

That's why we need everybody in the theological game, around the world, at all levels, all races and cultures, along the sexual spectrum and gender continuum. But, even together, even with the witness of Jesus and the inspiration of the Holy Spirit, what we come up with is going to look like a child's drawing of God. (No offense to children intended.)

As I look out at the old, magnificent trees behind my home or up at the stars far above those trees, I stretch my imagination to consider the God beyond human knowledge, the infinite beyond the finite. But I can't even imagine it.

Forgive my audacity, O God, to believe even my thoughts can contain you!

THURSDAY, SECOND WEEK OF LENT

> *O God, …*
>   *my soul thirsts for you;*
> *my flesh faints for you,*
>   *as in a dry and weary land where there is no*
>   *water.*
> Psalm 63:1

What a needy, desperate character this Psalmist is! Doesn't he have any friends? Can't she get a life?

It may be hard to imagine someone so centrally focused on God in our society, in which God serves us like an additive in our fuel, a vitamin enrichment for our cereal, or one more friend to call on.

We who have been in the wilderness betwixt liberation and the Promised Land may enjoy a keener sense of our thirsty need for God, but we have a lot of distractions in our wilderness. Can we really trust Moses? Is it appropriate for Miriam to dance? How will we have enough manna for retirement when we barely get enough to last us a day? Will we find another watering hole before our water jars are empty?

God is more than an added attraction at life's amusement park. More than getting a life, we need to get God.

O God, my soul thirsts for you; my flesh faints for you, as in a dry and weary land where there is no water.

FRIDAY, SECOND WEEK OF LENT

> *God works vindication*
> *and justice for all who are oppressed.*
> Psalm 103:6

Hard to believe that's true. Especially when God's *people* neither vindicate us nor give us justice.

Christians are better with every other justice issue than with the lesbian, gay, bisexual, transgender one. Many conservative Christians actually feel pious and holy when they batter us. Many liberal Christians actually feel pious and holy when they don't. I'd trade in all such liberal Christian friends for those who would risk their vocations and their church for our vindication and justice. As it is, more often the ones willing to risk our church's life to save it are those who oppose us.

But this is changing. Ministers are being defrocked for blessing same-gender marriages. Congregations are being disfellowshipped for affirming our membership, ministries, and marriages. Families are leaving nonwelcoming churches and joining ones that welcome their gay family member. This reaffirms to me that Christianity is a movement rather than an institution, that Christians are truly people of The Way, as scripture calls them, rather than people of The System.

It's time for more Christians to get moving. To be The Way or get out of the way so the Spirit can do her work.

Move me, shape me, fill me, use me—Spirit of the living God, fall afresh on me.

SATURDAY, SECOND WEEK OF LENT

> *Nevertheless with most of them God was not pleased; for they were overthrown in the wilderness.* 1 Corinthians 10:5

Paul reminds the church at Corinth of the temptations the Hebrews endured in the wilderness after their liberation from Egypt. He puts the Corinthians' griping in perspective: "No temptation has overtaken you that is not common to every one. God is faithful, and will not let you be tempted beyond your strength; but with the temptation God will also provide the way of escape, so that you may be able to endure it" (10:13).

All kinds of temptations bombard us in the wilderness of heterosexism. The temptation to give up. The temptation to go back to Egypt, perhaps not to slavery, but to security of one kind or another. The temptation to make the wilderness our way of life, to forever live with a survivor's (or victim's) mentality. The temptation to accept a theology of scarcity when it comes to God's grace. The temptation to stay at an oasis rather than proceed to the Promised Land. The temptation to worship something other than God to make life easier: drugs, alcohol, sex, a lover, our movement, even our deprivation or martyrdom. The temptation to compete with others regarding how much we've suffered.

The spiritual life requires a wilderness, I believe—an opportunity to rely wholly on God and discern who God calls us to be. But wilderness is to God's realm what strategy is to goal and what discipline is to accomplishment. Those who fall in the wilderness may lose touch with their purpose, for anticipating the result of our efforts makes even the wilderness blossom.

Lead me not into temptation; but deliver me from evil.

THIRD SUNDAY IN LENT

> *"And if it bears fruit next year, well and good; but
> if not, you can cut it down."* Luke 13:9

Jesus said this about the next decision-making gathering of
your denomination or tradition.

Well, *why not?*

Jesus said the of an unfruitful fig tree that its owner wants
toppled. But the vinedresser (Jesus?) basically says, "Let me
work with it some more, put some more manure on it, and
see if next year it bears fruit. If not, then we'll cut it down."

Seems as if the church gets steeped in manure every year,
and yet it holds onto fruitless policies denying the gifts
and relationships of lesbian, gay, bisexual, and transgender
people. And we're such *good* fruit!

The policies are fruitless for another reason: they have a
broader message. "No," our churches say, "We're not going to
behave as Jesus did, embracing those who have been spiritually abused and socially outcast." If our churches don't welcome gay people, then others might not be welcome either,
because they're divorced, disabled, different, single, poor,
uneducated, whatever.

These days, the Magic Kingdom is closer to the commonwealth of God.

*God of justice, may the church follow the moral and spiri-
tual leadership of municipalities and businesses that have
nondiscrimination policies and domestic partner benefits.*

MONDAY, THIRD WEEK OF LENT

And Jesus laid his hands upon her, and immedi-
ately she was made straight, and she praised God.
Luke 13:13

Since our opposition often takes the Bible so literally, it's a wonder they haven't used this text in their arguments for "healing" homosexuals!

Once again, Jesus raises a ruckus by healing on the sabbath day, this time a woman with an eighteen-year infirmity that bent her back.

Bernadette Brooten, author of the landmark book *Love Between Women*, co-led a conference with Janie Spahr and me several years ago. As a Catholic teaching Christianity at a largely Jewish university (Brandeis), she commented to me how interesting it is to get her Jewish students' viewpoints on Jesus. "Why didn't Jesus just heal the people on the next day," some of them have questioned, "rather than causing controversy by doing it on the sabbath?"

Makes sense. But he healed on other days as well. He just happened to see her on the sabbath. What if another opportunity never arose?

Our own sacred day of Sunday is frequently an opportunity to heal those whose backs have been bent by unseen spiritual burdens, by homophobia, by racism, by fundamentalism, by biblical literalism, by economic injustice, by gender expectations, by sexism. Think how ministers are regarded who follow Jesus' lead and attempt to heal these folk on our own sabbath through sermons and liturgies and church school classes! Troublemakers, all. Like Jesus.

Dear Jesus, heal the church bent by legalism, so it may better praise God!

TUESDAY, THIRD WEEK OF LENT

And God said to Joshua, "This day I have rolled away the reproach of Egypt from you." Joshua 5:9

Having arrived in the Promised Land and tasted the firstfruits of their victory, the produce of the land of Canaan, scripture tells us "the people of Israel had manna no more." This kind of makes me sad. Having never lived on "manna," whatever it was, I can afford some nostalgia for it. The Hebrews, in reality, were probably sick to death of it!

In our wilderness, I wonder what our "manna" is. Whatever it is, I believe our menu is more varied. Scripture. Sacraments. Encouraging sermons. Welcoming churches. Newsletters and gatherings of our denomination's LGBT organization. Affirming books.

We'd like to live to the day when we can be nostalgic for all these things. To see us all in some LGBT Christian retirement community laughing and crying about the way things were.

But what will it mean to have the "reproach" of the church and society rolled away from us? God, I'd sure like to enjoy that feeling. You may have to tie a kite string on me.

God, in this moment, lighten my burdens, to have a taste of ultimate freedom as your child!

WEDNESDAY, THIRD WEEK OF LENT

> *While I kept silence, my body wasted away*
> *through my groaning all day long.*
> *For day and night your hand was heavy upon me;*
> *my strength was dried up as by the heat of*
> *summer.*
> Psalm 32:3–4

The Psalmist continues, writing that all this changed when acknowledging the Psalmist's sin. All of this began to change for us when we acknowledged our sin of silence, our sin of accepting others' prejudice, our sin of refusing to embrace the sacred nature of our love.

The broader church wonders why it groans in controversy, its membership wasting away, feeling the weight of the hand of God on its heart, often enervated in its mission of proclaiming the gospel.

As we, the whole church, acknowledge our sin, the sin of silence at injustice, the sin of adopting society's prejudice, the sin of refusing to embrace and celebrate the sacred nature of gay love—then we all may "shout for joy" and "be glad in the LORD" (Psalm 32:11).

May our strength be renewed as the eagle's! May we soar and not be weary in doing what is right for the good of all!

THURSDAY, THIRD WEEK OF LENT

All this is from God, who through Christ reconciled us to God's self and gave us the ministry of reconciliation. 2 Corinthians 5:18

The theme of reconciliation in its Confession of 1967 is what clinched it for me that I belonged in the Presbyterian Church. I had been searching for a more open church than the fundamentalist, biblical-literalist one in which I'd been reared. I wanted a church that took the authority of scripture to heart by utilizing biblical scholarship as well as Spirit-guided meditation to discover its truths. I hoped for a church that promoted equality and reconciliation in the local and global community. I had not yet accepted my sexuality, but my sense of being different undoubtedly enhanced my view that reconciliation is central to the gospel message.

Many of my fellow Presbyterians will be aghast, but the Presbyterian Church helped me reconcile my sexuality and my spirituality. My home Presbyterian congregation asked me to help with a forum on sexuality for their youth, long before I had accepted my own sexuality, and I realized sexuality was not a taboo topic in my new church as it had been in my Baptist one. Later, when I suggested a forum for the whole congregation with representatives of the largely gay Metropolitan Community Church, the minister and elders agreed to it and the congregation attended in record numbers. And a Presbyterian study document, "Sexuality and the Human Community," new at the time, seemed to hold a compassionate if not quite accepting view of homosexuality. These proved to be the beginnings of reconciliation for my Christian faith and my homosexuality.

The LGBT group and welcoming congregations program in each Christian tradition and denomination have lived out a ministry of reconciliation. Two such programs have even taken the word to name their churches—United Methodists have Reconciling congregations—and Lutherans have Reconciling in Christ congregations. It has grieved us that our ministries of reconciliation have prompted others to engage in harsh rhetoric and acts of separation, division, condemnation, and exclusion.

Our opponents charge that we are trying to divide the church, the Body of Christ, when, in truth, we are trying to heal the Body of Christ of its brokenness, not just between gay and straight, but over issues of spirituality and sexuality, the biblical word and the Word made flesh, God's grace and human legalism, the institutional church and the movement of the Holy Spirit.

Make me an ambassador of Christ's reconciliation in the church and the world. Amen.

FRIDAY, THIRD WEEK OF LENT

> *But while he was yet at a distance, his father saw*
> *him and had compassion, and ran and embraced*
> *him and kissed him.* Luke 15:20

When Henri Nouwen contemplated this parable of the prodigal in Rembrandt's painting *The Return of the Prodigal Son,* he first thought of himself as the younger son, having gone far from the family home in Holland to find himself and his ministry largely in North America. He was aware of his own deep need for forgiveness, and the gracious, loving arms of a father God who would welcome him home.

But as he contemplated, he realized that he was also the elder brother, literally the eldest in his family who had done everything that was expected of him, becoming a priest, and sometimes resenting the freedom of his younger siblings. He became aware of his own unforgivingness, and the resentment he felt for the grace shown even those who hadn't turned out as expected.

In conversation with a nun in his community, however, he experienced another startling revelation as he described himself to her as both prodigal and elder brother. She said to him, "But, Henri, we need you to be our father!" In other words, he now was called to assume the role of the forgiver, welcoming other "prodigals" home, entreating the elder brother to join the celebration.

This may parallel our own reception of the story. Many of us felt we had to leave home to become ourselves, to acknowledge our identities. Others of us were the very responsible elder siblings who remained behind, caring for our parents or our families. But many of us fail to think of ourselves becoming the forgiving father or mother who reaches out with a hug and a kiss to welcome all of our family, both outside and within the church.

Yet, if we are to imitate God as the forgiving parent, we are called to offer forgiveness, reaching out to the runaway and reconciling the resistant.

Let's run down that road, let's go out to entreat, and welcome our children home.

Forgive us our debts and trespasses as we forgive our debtors and trespassers.

SATURDAY, THIRD WEEK OF LENT

I will make a way in the wilderness. Isaiah 43:19

I think we forget that the wilderness *is* the way.

Since first being tossed out of Eden on our ear and having to make it on our own by laboring in the soil of the wilderness, we've discovered more about ourselves than the forbidden tree could ever teach us. And one of the things we've discerned is that God was right: the harmony and communion of the Garden is the better way to live. No wonder the prophets talk about the blossoming of the desert as the fulfillment of God's time.

The wilderness is the way toward discovering what's truly vital to life. Communion. Community. Calling.

Our world tries to tell us that the mystical experience is possible without discipline, that human solidarity is accessible without suffering, that one's true vocation is materially rewarded. But the desert teaches us that we must marshal our energies to continue the trek, that reaching to help a fallen companion means risk, and that vocation may mean sacrificing everything we have.

May my own wilderness shape, color, and fire my soul as your work of art, O God!

FOURTH SUNDAY IN LENT

> *When God restored the fortunes of Zion,*
> *we were like those who dream.*
> Psalm 126:1

With what relish the Psalmist celebrates the good turn of events for the people of Israel! But wait. The final verses of the Psalm reveal that this is a memory, not a present reality. The Psalmist in effect prays to God, "Do it again!"

Most of us have a memory of God answering our prayers in a way that was life-giving or love-restoring, like a dream. If we do not, our collective memory stored in scripture has many such instances. Drawing on such recollections forms the basis for our faith. The God who has realized our dreams, as individuals or as community, may give us what we hope for now.

God has realized dreams a lot more difficult than the acceptance and affirmation of lesbian, gay, bisexual, and transgender people! So let's begin, even in the desert, to fill our mouths with laughter and our tongues with shouts of joy!

Our God has done great things for us, and we rejoice!
(based on Psalm 126)

MONDAY, FOURTH WEEK OF LENT

> *If anyone else has reason to be confident in the flesh, I have more.* Philippians 3:4

The apostle Paul thus begins a description of how he has all the fleshly credentials to recommend him to God: he is heterosexual, a Christian cradle to grave and of many generations, a member of the Christian Coalition, a zealous persecutor of gay people, and one who has never broken a rule in the Bible. (This, of course, is the contemporary equivalent of his experience!)

And yet he counts that as sewage (a better translation of Philippians 3:8) when compared to "knowing Christ Jesus my Lord." He knows that nothing can save him except the grace of God manifested in Christ Jesus. No matter how well or in what way he performs for God, that's not what will save him and the relationship he has with God.

There are books called *The Joy of Lesbian Sex* and *The Joy of Gay Sex* and, for straight people, *The Joy of Sex.* These books offer techniques for lovemaking. The Bible could very well be called *The Joy of Jewish Spirituality* or *The Joy of Christian Spirituality.* The Bible offers techniques for loving God.

What's important with any of these manuals, however, is that we not confuse the techniques with the love. The love, as Paul points out, supersedes any skills for expressing that love. The love is what saves us in any relationship, not the techniques—whether with another person or with God.

This delivers us from performance anxiety!

And it frees us—just as it did Paul—to love God in new ways.

Free me to love you in new ways every day, dear God—never complacent with pride and never constrained by fear.

TUESDAY, FOURTH WEEK OF LENT

Mary took a pound of costly ointment of pure nard and anointed the feet of Jesus and wiped his feet with her hair; and the house was filled with the fragrance of the ointment. John 12:3

In this reminiscence of the story, the villain Judas is given the role of decrying Mary's action. In other versions, the critical comments are more general among Jesus' disciples.

I can't help but place today's Christians in this scene. The sensual nature of Mary's adoration would drive most Christians to distraction, but they would instead comment on the waste of money that could have been better used in evangelism or feeding the poor. Safer.

During a few of the retreats I've led, I've invited people to pair up and wash each other's feet. The intimacy of doing so made a *married* couple extremely uncomfortable, while two single people ended up in a passionate relationship!

Imagine being that intimate with the savior of humanity! Stroking his feet, cleaning his toenails with our fingertips, putting our face to the floor to rub the soles of his feet with our heads. Moreover, imagine Jesus allowing us to touch him so intimately.

One doesn't have to "reimagine" or "re-vision" God to disconcert the spiritually prudish. One has only to enter the story of the Bible in which God has already been imaged as a vulnerable, lovesick Creator and Messiah, hungry for our love, thirsty for our friendship, pleasuring in our touch.

Dear Jesus, let me love your body and may I let you love mine.

WEDNESDAY, FOURTH WEEK OF LENT

The Lord GOD has given me
the tongue of a teacher,
that I may know how to sustain
the weary with a word.
Isaiah 50:4

Think about a letter you received from someone who cares for you when you were feeling down-and-out. Or a phone call from a really good friend during a difficult period. Or an issue of a gay Christian newsletter just when you weren't feeling confident of your church connection.

Words are a way of being there for someone, a way of intimacy, that often goes far beyond mere physical presence. Haven't you sometimes felt closer to a friend when writing her a letter, or when lifting him in the words of a prayer?

At the top of a series of cutout quotes pasted above my work space is one in my mother's hand: "Let not adversity frighten you." I found the scrap of paper among her things after her death. She must've heard them in a sermon, or read them in a book, and copied the words that had brought her hope in a weary time. Now they sustain me, all the more significantly because they came from my first teacher.

Beyond "giving up" for Lent the time required to read these meditations, consider giving up a few words to someone in a letter, call, e-mail, or prayer—today, and the remaining days of Lent. Maybe words of affirmation and encouragement to leaders who have given of themselves in our struggle, or words of thanks and appreciation to family members and friends who have been supportive. And consider writing a story, article, reflection, or prayer for the newsletter of your denomination's LGBT group, or one of your denomination's churchwide publications, or an op-ed piece for your local newspaper or gay magazine.

Don't let Hallmark have all the fun.

Give us the gift of words—to speak, to write, to articulate a message of hope to cheer others.

THURSDAY, FOURTH WEEK OF LENT

> *O give thanks to the Lord, for God is good;*
>> *God's steadfast love endures forever!*
> *Blessed is the one who comes in the name of the*
>> *Lord.*
>> *We bless you from the house of God.*
> Psalm 118:1, 26

Henri Nouwen wrote of the minister (every Christian) as *The Living Reminder* of Christ, as one who re-presents God's steadfast love. Think how *mis*represented God's steadfast love has become, when we find ourselves suspicious of many "who come in the name of the Lord" and when we doubt that the house of God will bless us.

We must not assume that clergy and other Christians come in the name of God. Some do represent and incarnate God's steadfast love. But many are too busy representing themselves, or the institution they serve, or interests that counter or contradict Christ's steadfast love.

We must also be attentive to those who come in the name of God "unofficially," proclaiming God's steadfast love for us without benefit of training, ordination, church membership, or commitment to Christian dogma. Sometimes the living reminder of Christ comes as a stranger, as a pet, as a flower, as a lover.

Remember, Christ came first as a stranger, then as a teacher, then as a friend, and finally as a sacrificial lover willing to lay down his life. So certain were those he met that he had come in God's name that they called him "Child of God."

People of the Rainbow first seemed strangers to the church, but have quickly become teachers, been revealed as friends, and risked lives out of love for the church. We have tried to serve as living reminders of Christ. May the church come to say of us collectively, "Blessed is the one who comes in the name of the Lord."

As stranger, teacher, friend, and lover, God, bless me that I may bless others.

FRIDAY, FOURTH WEEK OF LENT

> *I am the* LORD, *that is my name;*
> *my glory I give to no other,*
> *nor my praise to idols.*
> Isaiah 42:8

The Inclusive Language Lectionary changes *Lord* to *Sovereign*. The connotations for me in Lord are softer than the connotations of Sovereign, and before the feminist movement I never associated it with maleness, as in "lords and ladies." The substitute "Sovereign" sounds severe. I wish there were another word altogether.

But the truth of the matter is that God is Sovereign. Jesus was coming to terms with that in his forty-day fast in the wilderness. I don't believe most of us have come to terms with this understanding of God. We like our images of a softer, gentler God. But God is a fierce mother who will defend her progeny to the death. And without her, we would not have been born, we would have no breasts on which to suckle, we would have no spiritual lap in which to rest. She's in charge, perhaps no longer the punitive father ready to beat us with a stick, but nonetheless one whose stern and just look reprimands our unloving behavior.

Perhaps we've needed the image of God as our friend to overcome the spiritually abusive, punitive-parent image. But God is not simply our friend. God is our soul friend, that is, our spiritual director. There is no equality to be had with God. God is above us, beyond us, outside of us, and deeper inside of us than we can ever go on our own. We are a part of God, but only a part.

Lent is a good time to get over ourselves and into God.

Sovereign God, keep me from thinking of myself more highly than I ought.

SATURDAY, FOURTH WEEK OF LENT

> *[All people may] feast on the abundance of your*
> *house,*
> *   and you give them drink from the river of your*
> *   delights.*
> Psalm 36:7–8

In most houses of God, feasting and abundance, drinking and delight, are rarely a part of the worship of God. Especially during the period of Lent, sober, somber, and even dismal attitudes are considered a reverent and proper response to God.

But anyone who has fasted more than three days knows that one can get downright giddy going without food that long. Longer fasting can bring on hallucinations, much like the religious use of peyote by some Native Americans. At the least, other sensations come to the fore, and one may forget one's hunger in amnesiac bliss. (Though one may also go "postal" out of hunger!)

Near-death experiences may be the result of a similar euphoria as the brain is deprived of oxygen and other nutrients needed to transact the business of life.

Many religions practice forms of deprivation to locate or discern the spiritual realm. These may afford the disciple a form of spiritual pleasure. But if they simply involve or intend suffering, a disciple may forget the pleasure that God offers. One who has not known pleasure in at least some small way has not known God. Our call as evangelicals is to make pleasure more widely available to all—the poor, the marginalized, the oppressed—though often we find *they* are the ones to teach *us* pleasure!

May I be both a good and a thankful steward of your pleasure, incarnate God, rather than regard it as less than your gift.

FIFTH SUNDAY IN LENT

Do not cast me off in the time of old age;
*   forsake me not when my strength is spent.*
Psalm 71:9

We like old people who "don't act their age." So old people who are tired, alone, or face disabilities and immobilities acquired as the body ages are often forgotten, abandoned, ignored.

We see this ourselves when the new generation "takes charge" of things in which we've been involved. Younger people may act as if we never existed, as if we never prepared the way for them, as if our collective history began with them, as if we are no longer a part of "their" community.

This gives us the opportunity to enter a new wilderness, letting go of our earlier existence, involvements, history, and community and, like the desert hermits of the ancient church, discovering a new relationship with God.

How foolish we will be, however, if we fail to notice that this new wilderness is already populated with wise old sages who offer insights as well as laughter, pleasure as well as spiritual guidance.

Thank you, Most Ancient of Days, for sages who inhabit our wilderness and inspire our faith.

MONDAY, FIFTH WEEK OF LENT

> *Consider your own call, brothers and sisters.*
> 1 Corinthians 1:26

The Inclusive Language Lectionary substitutes "my friends" for the "brethren" of the old Revised Standard Version. Translationwise and theologically, the phrase "brothers and sisters" used by the New Revised Standard Version is more appropriate than either of the earlier choices. The family of Christian faith, following Jesus' lead, began early on to call one another sister and brother, in a community in which women as well as men were vital. It indicated our *permanent* place in the spiritual family, whereas the status of a friend may change, being dependent on mere feelings or mere agreement of belief and behavior.

Usually when we read this verse we revel in what follows: "Not many of you were wise ... powerful ... noble." But rather than think of ourselves as stupid, weak, hated, and nothing, I think that, without assigning any worth or value to ourselves based on worldly competition, we should simply consider our call.

Collectively, our unique position in the world and the church qualifies us to add much to the life of the church, restoring eros (the passion for intimacy, thus honesty and integrity, with God and with others) to the disembodied Milquetoast spirituality that prefers ignorance for the sake of institutional survival, rejects inclusiveness for the sake of individual comfort, and denies justice for the sake of ritual purity.

Eros has mistakenly been separated from agape in our thinking and the two have even been treated as opposites.

But agape without eros is an effete caricature of the love that Jesus practiced; otherwise he would never have given up his body in his Passion, nor would he have been required to do so by the political and religious authorities of his time. Eros puts our body on the line in the service of agape. When the church does likewise, together we can move on to other issues.

Blend the passion of eros and the grace of agape in my spirituality, Passionate Lover of my soul.

TUESDAY, FIFTH WEEK OF LENT

> *Let those be put to shame and confusion*
> *who seek my life.*
> Psalm 70:2

Years ago a Christian ally told me that she thought that Christians resisted giving justice to gays and lesbians because they had not been adequately shamed for their injustice. I accepted her intent and insight, but inwardly I doubted both the concept and wisdom of a shame-based system of correction.

The Psalmist entertained no such qualms. The Psalmist also did not exercise the restraint of Gandhi and King in referring to *enemies* as *the opposition*, a practice I have imitated, which is intended to avoid dehumanizing or demonizing the opponent.

Opening a gay support group with a devotion based on Psalm 69, with many references to enemies, a seminarian said she never understood what the Psalmist meant by *enemies* until she came out as a lesbian in the church.

We have people who have made themselves our enemies. They seek our life in the Body of Christ and in the body politic. They are already working from confusion and shame about sexuality—theirs and ours. Since I firmly believe that some reconciliation will never occur on this side of the commonwealth of God, we can only pray with the Psalmist that others will see their shame and that their strategy will continue to be confused.

Let those be put to shame and confusion who seek my life.

WEDNESDAY, FIFTH WEEK OF LENT

> *Let us run with perseverance the race that is set before us, looking to Jesus the pioneer and perfecter of our faith, who for the sake of the joy that was set before him endured the cross, disregarding its shame.* Hebrews 12:1–2

Jewish law declared, "Anyone hung on a tree is under God's curse" (Deuteronomy 21:23). Crucifixion was a humiliating death by exposure, the same fate as the scapegoat sent off into the wilderness to die after the sins of the people had been projected onto it by the high priest on the annual Day of Atonement. Yet Jesus' faithfulness and God's will transformed the shame of the cross into the vindication and joy of the resurrection.

We have been cursed, shamed, and excommunicated. But that's the will of the religious and political authorities, not the will of God. So God has vindicated us and blessed us with joy in our resurrection: in gay neighborhoods and relationships and friends and extended families, in gay and lesbian groups, pride marches and festivals, in a growing bisexual community, in an emerging transgendered community, in LGBT Christian networks and inclusive congregations.

More and more, it is clearly members of our opposition who are twisted with their own cursing, humiliated by their own shaming, and buried in their own whitewashed tombs.

If only they could hear Jesus' call to Lazarus: "Come out!"

Let me run with perseverance, looking to Jesus the pioneer and perfecter of my faith, for the sake of the joy of resurrection beyond whatever opponents try to do to me.

THURSDAY, FIFTH WEEK OF LENT

> *I will put my law within them, and I will write it*
> *upon their hearts; and I will be their God, and*
> *they shall be my people.* Jeremiah 31:33

God promises this new covenant because the people broke
the old one "though I was married to them," God declares.

As central and significant as Torah was, the prophets
repeatedly reminded the people that what counted most
was what was going on in their hearts. Rationalizations could
argue one out of the responsibility of caring for one's parents or even one's wife, Jesus pointed out, both responsibil-
ities demanded by the law. Self-righteousness could easily
stem from following the letter of the law while ignoring its
spirit, both Jesus and the apostle Paul pointed out.

The addition to our own denominational Torahs of antigay statements is not half so significant as what was going on
in the hearts of those who championed them. They were
intent on keeping us out, claiming the church is only for
those with a heterosexual orientation. Moreover, they idola-
trously believe that heterosexuality is the condition of
entrance into God's commonwealth rather than faith in Jesus
Christ. Whatever improvements might be made to our
denominational polities and policies in coming years still are
not so important as what is in the hearts of Christians who
will still retain an antigay prejudice.

Rationalizations and self-righteousness will continue to
be the order of the Christian day until more Christians truly
accept Jesus into their hearts as the new covenant, the law
written upon our hearts.

Write your law upon my heart! You are my God, and I belong to you.

FRIDAY, FIFTH WEEK OF LENT

> *What shall I render to the Lord*
> *for all God's bounty to me?*
> *I will lift up the cup of salvation*
> *and call on the name of the Lord.*
> Psalm 116:12–13

When my family said grace for a meal at a restaurant, my brother would be under the table "looking for his napkin" out of embarrassment. Though my parents' doing so was sincere and natural for them, I do not like to pray in restaurants, because it feels to me like a public display of piety. Instead, I have taken to toasting God: "Thanks be to God." In an ethnic restaurant I might elaborate, "Thanks be to God for Mexican people and Mexican food!" referring to whatever the particular origin of the food.

In his book *Can You Drink the Cup?* Henri Nouwen wrote about three distinct movements of the spiritual life, using the cup as metaphor. Holding the cup is contemplating one's life. Lifting the cup is offering a blessing of one's life to others. Drinking the cup is receiving life with all its sorrows and joys. All the movements are part of thanksgiving, or Eucharist.

We have much to be thankful for. We have been given much, we have much to offer others as a blessing, and we have many sorrows and joys to savor. Lent may be a season for holding, lifting, and drinking our cup. To life!

Thanks be to God for all I have been given and all who have given to me!

SATURDAY, FIFTH WEEK OF LENT

> *Let us draw near with a true heart in full assur-*
> *ance of faith, with our hearts sprinkled clean*
> *from an evil conscience and our bodies washed*
> *with pure water.* Hebrews 10:22

As a teenager, before I realized the sacred gift of my sexuality, I used my showers as an opportunity to wash away
my "sins" symbolically, vowing never again to think *those*
thoughts and never again to pleasure myself sexually.

As adults, many of us have not always remembered the
sacred nature of our sexuality. While sex may be recreational
and re-creational, our sexuality has sometimes not led us to
treat ourselves and others as sacred, as loving, and as lovable.
We may carry regrets, sadness, and grief.

All the more we need to hear the writer of Hebrews
reflecting on the Jeremiah passage quoted Thursday, which
includes the assurance of God, "I will remember their sins
and their misdeeds no more" (Jeremiah 31:34). As we wan-
der in the wilderness with Jesus in search of the commonwealth of God, we need to let go of the dross of our lives that
hangs on to us, that prevents us from rising to our true nature
as beloved sons and daughters of God. If God is willing to let
it go, how much more should we!

Sprinkle my conscience clean, Holy God; wash from my
body sin that clings so closely.

PALM SUNDAY

> *As Jesus was now drawing near, at the descent of*
> *the Mount of Olives, the whole multitude of the*
> *disciples began to rejoice and praise God with a*
> *loud voice for all the mighty works that they had*
> *seen.* Luke 19:37

Fickle folk. They would subsequently doubt Jesus, question his authority, test him, plot against him, deny him, betray him, arrest him, and demand his crucifixion.

We have a small taste of Jesus' experience. Many of us have served our community or our church in such a way that those who knew us would "praise God with a loud voice for all the mighty works that they had seen." Yet coming out could bring, or has brought, the various negative reactions that Jesus suffered. People have doubted us, questioned our authority, tested us, plotted against us, denied us, betrayed us, arrested us, and demanded our sacrifice.

One could say the destructive reactions to Jesus resulted from the people's disillusionment. But that implies that what they saw in Jesus was an illusion of God's presence among them. Rather, I believe, it was a vision of God's presence among them that they later doubted, questioned, betrayed, and denied.

The destructive reactions we endure result from a similar loss of vision among those who initially viewed us as beloved children of God. But they also originate in the culture and the church's illusion that beloved children of God are straight.

"Where there is no vision, the people perish," Proverbs 29:18 (KJV) says.

Restore our vision, God, that we may live.

MONDAY OF HOLY WEEK

Jesus said, " ... The poor you always have with you,
but you do not always have me." John 12:8

Jesus said this defending Mary's anointing him with a costly balm. It seems a strange thing to say for someone who devoted his life to the poor.

Years ago, a friend considered a call to serve among the poor of Latin America. I sensed that part of his attraction to this ministry was its acceptability over against serving those in his very own gay community. I challenged him by saying that if I were a person coping with AIDS, I would want him by my side as a gay Christian minister.

A minister with a liberal political agenda told me that he could not be openly supportive of gay members in his congregation or he would never be able to accomplish his goals of justice. Huh?

A church leader with an evangelical agenda once said to me that homosexuals coming into the church would keep people from joining. Come again?

Seems to me that we should anoint whoever is in our midst, whether it's the poor or Jesus or lesbians, gay men, bisexuals, or transgenders! You never know how long any of us is going to be here.

May I anoint others with love this day, for I may not have
another opportunity.

TUESDAY OF HOLY WEEK

*Now among those who went up to worship at the
feast were some Greeks. So these came to Philip ...
and said, "Sir, we wish to see Jesus."* John 12:20–21

Oddly, we never find out if the Greeks ever got to see Jesus.
I remember a preacher telling the story of a well-known
preacher who kept before him in the pulpit the words, "We
would see Jesus!"

"We would see Jesus!"

These words should be carved on the inside of every pulpit, the table of every delegate to a national and regional
church assembly and church court, embossed on every book
of polity, framed on a wall where a congregation's council
meets, hung as a banner over every congregational meeting.

"We would see Jesus!"

This should become the mantra of every Sunday school
teacher, every church staff person, every church service
provider, every Christian everywhere.

Remembering that the plea came from Greeks, who were
morally unacceptable and ritually unclean Gentiles, we
might manifest Jesus to the very outcasts he chose as his own
companions.

May others see Jesus in what I do or say.

WEDNESDAY OF HOLY WEEK

> *Jesus was troubled in spirit, and testified, "Truly,*
> *truly, I say to you, one of you will betray me."* John
> 13:21

This reminds me of Jesus' reaction to the death of his beloved friend Lazarus two chapters earlier in John: "he was greatly disturbed in spirit and deeply moved." Betrayal is like a death. Many of us who have been leaders in our movement have been or have felt betrayed at one time or another. We have been betrayed by those who remained silent when we anticipated they would speak in our defense. We have been betrayed by those to whom we confided a strategy, who used the information to counter our moves.

Closer to home, we have been betrayed by those whose ambition made our movement another arena of competition. We have been betrayed by those whose anger and self-hatred got projected onto us. We have been betrayed by those whose expectations or standards we did not live up to.

Jesus, of course, was innocent in a way we cannot claim to be. And Jesus suffered the ultimate betrayal, one that led to his death as well as that of his betrayer. Most of the betrayals we have endured have led "only" to the death of a friendship, an alliance, or at most, our vocation.

Yet, as Jesus was to experience resurrection at God's hand, so God is able to offer us resurrection. I have found reconciliation has been possible with many of the people by whom I've felt betrayed or who felt betrayed by me. Today we might consider those reconciliations that are possible on this side of the commonwealth of God. Reconciliation leads to new life for all involved.

*Inspire me, Jesus, to practice the forgiveness and the repen-
tance that lead to a resurrecting reconciliation.*

MAUNDY THURSDAY

> [Jesus said,] "I give you a new commandment, that you love one another. Just as I have loved you, you also should love one another. By this everyone will know that you are my disciples, if you have love for one another." John 13:34-35

If only Christians *did* love one another, the whole world would be saved. If only Christians and Jews and Muslims and Hindus and Sikhs and Buddhists and Wiccans and New Agers and New Thought practitioners and pagans and agnostics and atheists *did* love one another, the whole world would be at peace.

We all forget that we are all beloved by God, that we are all thus empowered to love others.

It's ironic that some heterosexual Christians want to muzzle homosexual and bisexual love. Seems like we need all the love we can get, in the church and the world. Why betray or deny or crucify that love because of sexual orientation? Why not serve one another as Jesus did, humbling ourselves to wash one another's feet, bringing cooling, refreshing waters to those feet, hot and tired and blistered from life's pilgrimage?

If you think about it, Jesus was rejected for his *spiritual* orientation of love.

May I wash not only fellow pilgrims' feet, but their hands and head as well!

GOOD FRIDAY

> *Surely this one has borne our griefs*
> *and carried our sorrows;*
> *yet we esteemed the servant stricken,*
> *smitten by God, and afflicted.*
> Isaiah 53:4

Blaming the victim is apparently as old as the Bible! The Suffering Servant was to bear our grief and sorrows, yet we assumed and assume that it is somehow the servant's responsibility, karma, or destiny. Later in the passage even the prophet concludes that "it was the will of God to bruise him and put him to grief" (v. 10).

Gimme a break. Rather, give God a break. God's will was that we *listen up* to Jesus, not beat him up! God's will at most was for Jesus to take the risk that we might behave like Nazis, which we did, and have done again and again over the centuries, crucifying the innocent because we project onto them our own inadequacy, sins, fear, hatred, and violence.

It's time to get over our bloodthirsty, sacrificial needs. While championing victims' rights, we need to end the death penalty. While supporting a woman's legal right to choose, we need to preach the choice of contraceptives over that of abortion. While encouraging family values, we need to end the destruction of gay people and gay families. While promoting self-determination and democracy throughout the world, we need to end our war making.

If one believes in the need for sacrificial victims, then at least one must admit there's been enough bloodshed on earth alone to save the universe! I think that's the atoning message of Jesus' crucifixion: Enough is enough! Stop, in the name of God, or else you might crucify God again!

Don't just forgive us, God, for we know not what we do— transform us!

> *After these things, Joseph of Arimathea, who was*
> *a disciple of Jesus, though a secret one because of*
> *his fear of the Jews, asked Pilate to let him take*
> *away the body of Jesus....Nicodemus, who had at*
> *first come to Jesus by night, also came, bringing*
> *a mixture of myrrh and aloes.* John 19:38–39

Those who wouldn't have been caught dead with Jesus in public and in daylight show up in private to anoint and bury a dead Jesus. There's some redemption in that, of course. But how much more they could have enjoyed their redemption if they'd been there earlier, with other disciples, who listened to his words, witnessed his healings, and ministered alongside!

We know Christians and Christian leaders who are supportive of us and our ministry privately. For fear of other Christians they do not acknowledge their support publicly. They hesitate to be with us and share our ministry.

A friend with AIDS told his family and friends that he would rather they came to visit him while he was healthy than wait until he was dying or dead. As needed as they would be then, he needed and wanted them in his everyday life, when they could enjoy one another's company to the fullest.

We will need our friends later, of course. But we need them *now* to speak up, to speak out *now*—not when it's too late.

Challenge our friends to be like Jesus, willing to lay down his life for us.

EASTER

Jesus said to her, "Mary!" She turned and said to him in Hebrew, "Rabbouni!" (which means Teacher).
John 20:16

Along with the disciple Mary, we know the resurrected Jesus because we have somehow heard him speak our name. He has called us personally to live the life he did, to minister in his name. He is as much alive to us as he was to Mary in that garden outside his tomb.

Many of our sisters and brothers have not heard Jesus speak their name, or have doubted his voice because the church has drowned out his message to them. Many of our lesbian daughters and gay sons and bisexual and transgender children may not hear Jesus speak their name. If we, as the Body of Christ, do not call them by name, they may not know Jesus. They may never experience the joy of Easter, God's desire to love us from death into life.

All we do must be for those who have not heard, who do not know the gospel story: that they are beloved children of God, created, redeemed, and nurtured by a God who calls them by name, reaching out to them as a mother hen gathers her brood under her wing, not wanting a single little one to be lost.

May I "feed your sheep," Jesus—especially the "other sheep" who are not in the church's fold.

Scripture Index

Includes both texts of the days as well as most texts referred to in the meditations themselves.

Nehemiah 8:9–12, Jan 26.

Esther 9:30, Jan 4.

Job 7:7, Feb 13, **7:16–18,** Jan 19, **38:4–7,** Jan 19.

Psalms 8:4–5, 9, Jan 19, **27:4,** Fr, Lent 1, **32:3–4, 11,** We, Lent 3, **36:7–8,** Sa, Lent 4, **40:9–10,** Jan 24, **51:12,** Th after Ash Wednesday, **63:1,** Th, Lent 2, **70:2,** Tu, Lent 5, **71:9,** Su, Lent 5, **73:2–12, 21–22,** Feb 19, **91:14,** Mo, Lent 1, **103:6,** Fr, Lent 2, **116:12–13,** Fr, Lent 5, **118:1, 26,** Th, Lent 4, **126:1, 3,** Su, Lent 4, **139:1, 3, 23–24,** Feb 18, **139:13,** Tu, Adv 1, **147:2–4,** Feb 8.

Proverbs 29:18, Psalm Sunday,

Ecclesiastes 5:12, Feb 29.

Isaiah 6:3–4, Feb 2, **6:5,** Feb 2, **11:6,** Fr, Adv 4, **40:3–4,** Jan 2, **42:8,** Fr, Lent 4, **43:6–8, 10,** Th, Adv 4, **43:19,** Sa, Lent 3, **49:3, 4, 6,** Mar 3, **50:4,** We, Lent 4, **53:4, 10,** Good Friday, **55:8,** We, Lent 2, **56:4–8,** Th, Adv 4; also Mar 4, **60:1, 5,** Jan 7.

Jeremiah 17:9–10, Feb 18, **31:33,** Th, Lent 5, **31:34,** Sa, Lent 5.

Daniel 9:22–23, Mo, Adv 1.

Joel 2:13, Ash Wednesday.

Micah 6:8, Jan 5, Feb 11.

Matthew 1:1, We, Adv 1, **1:20–21, 24,** Mo, Adv 4, **2:1–2,** Th, Adv 3, **2:10–11,** Jan 8, **2:16,** Dec 27, **2:23,** Mo, Adv 4, **3:16–17,** Jan 9, **4:17, 23,** Jan 10, **4:23,** Feb 10, **6:21,** Sat after Ash Wednesday, **10:16,** Sa, Adv 1, **10:26,** Tu, Adv 4, **10:37,** Wed, Adv 1, **11:16–19,** Dec 28, **11:28–30,** Dec 31, **12:22–32,** Th, Adv 3, **13:54–57,** Feb 28, **19:3–12,** Dec 30, **19:26,** Th, Adv 1, **22:1–2, 8–10,** Jan 27, **22:15–22,** Dec 26, **23:3–4,** Dec 30, **23:15,** Tu, Adv 4, **25:31–46,** Su, Lent 2, **26:26–28,** Feb 27, **27:50–51,** Feb 16, **28:16–17,** Feb 25, **28:19–20,** Fr, Adv 2; also Jan 4.

Mark 1:23–27, Jan 25, **1:35,** Feb 12, **1:40–41,** Feb 23, **3:28–29,** Tu, Adv 1, **3:32–35,** Mar 5; also We, Adv 1; Dec 29, **6:17–29,** Dec 27, **10:13–15,** Dec 27, **10:25, 27,** Su, Adv 4, **16:14,** Feb 25.

Luke 1:6, Sat, Adv 3, **1:19–20, 64–65,** Fr, Adv 3, **1:24–25,** Sat, Adv 3, **1:26–27,** Mo, Adv 1, **1:28–29,** Su, Adv 1, **1:35,** Tu, Adv 1; also Su, Adv 2, **1:41,** Christmas Eve, **1:46–49,** Su, Adv 3; also Su, Adv 4, **1:51,** Su, Adv 4, **2:1, 3–5,** Dec 26, **2:7,** Christmas, **2:8,** We, Adv 3, **2:30–31,** Tu, Adv 4, **2:34–35,** Tu, Adv 4; also Th, Adv 4, **2:36–38,** We, Adv 4, **2:46, 48–51,** Dec 29, **2:52,** Su, Adv 3, **3:4, 11,** Christmas Eve, **4:13,** We, Lent 1, **4:18–19,** Su, Adv 4, **5:1–11,** Feb 17, **6:3–4,** Mo, Adv. 3, **6:9,** Mo, Adv 3, **6:17, 20,** Jan 3, **9:28–29, 35,** Mar 7, **9:33,** Mo, Lent 2, **9:48,** Tu, Adv 4, **9:58,** Mo, Adv 2, **10:41–42,** Feb 6, **11:46,** Dec 30, **13:9,** Su, Lent 3, **13:13,** Mo, Lent 3, **13:34,** Fr, Adv 2, Jan 1, **13:35,** Su, Lent 2, **15:20,** Fr, Lent 3, **16:8,** Feb 7, **17:26–18:14,** Jan 2, **18:16,** Tu, Adv 4, **18:25, 27,** Jan 3, **19:37,** Palm Sunday, **19:41,** Fr, Adv 2, **24:11, 41,** Feb 25.

John 1:3–5, 9, Jan 5, **2:6–9,** Jan 11, **3:17,** Tu, Adv 2, **4:9,** Su, Adv 1, **4:21, 23,** Jan 5, **6:51, 59–61, 66,** Christmas, **9:3, 17, 41,** Th, Adv 4, **11:33, 35–36,** Fr, Adv 2, **12:3,** Tu, Lent 4, **12:8,** Mo, Holy Week, **12:20–21,** Tu, Holy Week, **13:21,** We, Holy Week, **13:34–35,** Maundy Th, **11:33, 35–36,** Fr, Adv 2, **15: 13–14,** Fr, Adv 2, **17:11,** Jan 28, **16:12–13,** Jan 30, **17:22–23,** Fr, Adv 2, **19:26–27,** Dec 29, **19:38–39,** Holy Sa, **20:16,** Easter, **20:25,** Feb 25, **20:29,** Christmas Eve, **21:4–6,** Feb 17.

Acts of the Apostles 2:4–6, Mar 6, **4:32,** Feb 9, **8:26–40,** Dec 31, **9:3–6,** Feb 4, **9:36–37, 39,** Feb 5, **10:15,** Jan 21, **10:35,** Mar 5, **10:45–47,** Jan 22.

Romans 4:3, We, Adv 1, **4:3, 22,** Mar 1, **5:6–21,** Dec 30, **8:22,** Jan 28, **10:11,** Tu, Lent 1, **12:1–2,** Jan 23, **12:4–6,** Jan 29.

1 Corinthians 1:4, 7, Feb 26, **1:10, 11–13,** Feb 9, **1:18, 25, 27; 3:18; 4:10,** Feb 20, **1:26,** Mo, Lent 5, **8:1–3,** Mar 2, **10:5, 13,** Sa, Lent 2, **10:30,** Mar 2, **12:12–13,** Jan 28, **12:24–26,** Jan 31, **13:5,** Feb 1, **13:12,** Su, Adv 3, **13:13,** Feb 1, **15:8–10,** Feb 15, **15:47, 49,** Dec 30.

2 Corinthians 1:18–20, Feb 24, **3:12–13, 17–18,** Jan 15, **3:18,** Mar 7, **5:18,** Th, Lent 3, **6:8–10,** Fr after Ash Wednesday.

Galatians 1:18, 2:1–6, Fr after Ash Wednesday, **3:28,** Jan 20.

Ephesians 2:8–10, Mar 1, **3:4–6,** Jan 6, Epiphany, **4:15–16,** Jan 30.

Philippians 2:12, 13, We, Adv 2, **3:4,** Mo, Lent 4, **3:13–14, 17,** Sa, Lent 1.